By David Bromige

The Gathering (1965)
Please, Like Me (1968)
The Ends of the Earth (1968)
The Quivering Roadway (1969)
Threads (1970)
Three Stories (1973)
Ten Years in the Making (1973)
Birds of the West (1974)
Tight Corners & What's Around Them (1974)
Out of My Hands (1974)
Spells & Blessings (1975)
Credences of Winter (1976)
Living in Advance [with deBarros and Gifford] (1976)
My Poetry (1980)
P-E-A-C-E (1981)
In the Uneven Steps of Hung-Chow (1982)
*It's the Same Only Different / The Melancholy Owed
    Categories* (1984)
You See, Parts 1 & 2 [with Opal Nations] (1986)
Red Hats (1986)
Desire: Selected Poems 1963–1987 (1988)

DAVID BROMIGE

DESIRE

SELECTED POEMS
1963-1987

BLACK SPARROW PRESS

SANTA ROSA  1988

The Western States Book Awards are a project of the Western States Arts Federation. The awards are supported by "Corporate Founder" The Xerox Foundation, Waldenbooks and Crane Duplicating Service. Additional funding is provided by the National Endowment for the Arts Literature Program.

Some of the poems in this book originally appeared in *The Gathering* (Sumbooks Press), *The Quivering Roadway* (Archangel Press), *Ten Years in the Making* (New Star Press), *Birds of the West* (The Coach House Press), *Spells & Blessings* (Talon Books), *My Poetry* (The Figures Press), *It's the Same Only Different / The Melancholy Owed Categories* (Last Straw Press) and *Red Hats* (Tonsure Press). Grateful acknowledgement is made to these publishers. Much of "Seeing That You Asked" is taken from questions Piaget posed to children, and their answers. "Able to Describe the Verses" owes a lot to Neruda's "lament." "Our Frequencies" is made from a list of the most frequently used English words. "Hieratics" incorporates passages from many more sources than I can cite here, but its principal borrowings are from Adorno's *Philosophy of Modern Music*, Marx's *18th Brumaire*, and Janson's *History of Art*. All the language of "The End of the Stranger" is taken from the final chapter of Camus' *L'Etranger*, in Stuart Gilbert's translation. The idea for a book somewhat like this turns out to have become I owe to Charles Simic; my thanks to him and to John Martin, who asked for it, and to Sara Anna, who typed the first version. None of this would exist at all had it not been for the support of a network of friends, acquaintances, readers and colleagues to each of whom, undying gratitude — you know who you are. And to Cecelia Belle — thanks, I don't know how you stand it. But I intend to stick around and find out.

Library of Congress Cataloging-in-Publication Data
Bromige, David, 1933
  Desire.

  I. Title.
PR9199.3.B696D4   1988   811'.54   88-3409
ISBN 0-87685-724-1
ISBN 0-87685-725-X (signed ed.)
ISBN 0-87685-723-3 (pbk.)

FOR CHRISTOPHER BROMIGE

of love's collision with desire begat
in July '63, and in Vancouver
when and where this book·began:

this longest (tallest) work of mine
has in its calendar kept time
with you in yours, and comforts

as you do — no doubt because I wrote it,
but what is more the point, thanks to
some quality all of its own, some entity

so decidedly not me looks back
and speaks what never had occurred
to me, and in this selfhood

sets forth, as the old stories say,
in quest of — oh, everything! — but
with luck, a like relief, content, delight.

12/16/87

Lacan was in fact always true to his own rules, which were neither capricious nor arbitrary. They were based on a Law that cannot be comprised by rules of civilized behavior, but that determines desire as the basis for action. This is the only path to the overcoming of narcissism, because desire is always the desire of the Other, as he put it, and because desire always seeks recognition by the Other's desire.

Love is far more impatient than desire; love demands love unconditionally and instantaneously; it demands what is commonly called instant gratification. People who commit suicide are lovers of death, and suicide is an act of love. . . . These acts represent a radical refusal to set forth on the path of desire.

Stuart Schneiderman, *Jacques Lacan*, pp. 22–24.

The posture called "tone" is a form of narrative irony.

James Rieger, *The Mutiny Within*, p. 164.

I keep screwing up in the same way. I just can't assimilate the fact that a lot of people out there could care less whether what they do is based on the results of thinking something through to the end. These dudes don't want to know about *certainty* as their numero uno need and they assume their angst comes from something else they can't afford. They can't even get it together to actively dislike someone who *does* ask the big questions of existence! Boy, do I find this contemptible! I guess that's how I get my kicks.

Nietzsche, *Die Fröhliche Wissenschaft*, 2nd edition, section 2, turned into Californian by D.B.

Table of Contents

Part One: Against Love

Part Two: Choosing the Event

Part Three: Watchers of the Skies

Part Four: The Art of Capitalism

Part Five: Typicality Enthralls with its Particular Failure

Part Six: Developing the Negative

DESIRE

PART ONE
Against Love

Revolving Door

Measured by ourselves alone, grief
overwhelms, it cannot be contained

without a larger scheme, as
fortune's wheel. He left her

in the hotel lobby, but can't
leave her alone, in his mind the light

her apartment window is
as he staggers home elsewhere late at night —

that they could make a kind of love
only last night, This,

our final kiss? waiting, waiting
for the airport bus, watched by

two fat suits, chuckling, Nice work
if you can get it, christ, you'd swear

misery shone, but each must be alone
in his loss, he walks blindly into

the revolving door, pushed as he
pushes, by a beauty, a call girl

maybe, or beloved hurrying to her lover
—a beginning? Or quite indifferent to

his wounded maleness, his or anybody
else's! the glass-&-wood wedge thrusts him

into the street, on his shoulder
the weight & force of those strange thighs.

With Someone Like You

"I tell you" who'd not inquired "I've forgotten
John, Arvids, Charlie, Ken, Walter
& that fascinating guy I met in
the Cosmopolitan Restaurant,"

as they sit down to her albums
the fire bright on her first
husband, arms akimbo in the Lake
District, & other pictures

she tears out & throws in the coals
fiercely as she embraces the present
seen in that light, representative.

At Last

Not the cracking of the ashtray on my
skull was the indicator but her
repeated scream, What do I want with a
husband — never once my name.

The ashtray was called Niagara
Falls & on our honeymoon, not spent
there, I was called
David in different accents
& responded differently.

But of all
the passionate scenes you may encounter
one when you stand for too
much, & that
is the indicator.

Affair of the Lemming

The ocean so still
under his thin skin, on

the snowy shore she
sees her dear face, & leaps

shattering skin & image &
not to go under, lashes about her.

Down in the Dance

"What was banished forever
I thought, laid by
lovers, by stages, by
friends spelling it out
for me returns

its clumsy legs to wear
mine out, its idiot
grin to spread
my face"

I'll drink it into the
ground, he cried, Even though
the monster & my awareness
of him be one & the same.

My Failing

Her eyes, the sheets her fingers
work over like lapels.

Morals, faded labels from foreign hotels
we slept in, our luggage.

How pretend nothing has happened
when precisely that is your conviction.

More

Sure I'll be your man again
when no one else is left alive —

you take my hand
& all the dead

sway by.

Taking Heart

Take me in again, how did I ever doubt
you were right for me, your mouth
beyond reproach, telling me you love me, your
    body is
an ocean, in its own way, saying the same—

so you lose, once more, giving me courage
to go away into the love of others,
lakes & rivers, surely
they will welcome
a body all of salt.

A Call

There is built a block in this city
which, when you get to it
very late into the night

first sight tells you every light is out
but can't stop making it
grow bigger, till

a door, you knock on, & nobody comes.
You thought you stood in the street, certainly
your legs were tired & cold, you thought

you lay asleep, up there, the warm
room the knock couldn't reach, your lips
relaxed, yet still

set, silent
as when you had seen them
earlier this evening.

You shouted, then, to the sky, you turned
over in bed, your head
half-buried in the pillow

to shut out those now
annoying noises from below — your mouth
as you saw it, closed

in a lovely smile.

A Choice Piece

Last night
here, there
tonight, tomorrow
with another

I see the statue
because you left this studio
I never finished, of you
slowly coming true.

The Quest

How lonesome I have been, for you.
Didn't you know — who
in this city I had built
to have some inexhaustible site
to go looking for you in,
hide, to my heart's fulfilment,
discontent.

Free & In Love?

Free & in love?
Driven speech!
Enslaved

by the given
arbitrarily
ennobled with
significance

as if the world
came to a point
& meaning

weren't a cruel mistress.

A Project

If only we carried our innards outside us
as sometimes less ostensibly complicated creatures.

If only he had to read the maze of my mysteries
before a decision had to be made. Loving isn't

long enough, bra slip & panties, he's on the lip
a panting ampersand, am I

then to deny, yet unready, o to lie
for aeons & load him with labors

the gods of old would have been proud they'd conceived!
O, pro tem, waiting for ideas to seize me, for those

long victorian dresses my grandfather
mentioned, eyeing my knees.

How to hold my head up striding down the street
& yet outdress his busy hands? we must

adorn ourselves like whores to make it
plain we're in the market, all the time

longing for infinite patience, infinite
fondling, preamble deep as a well with no bottom

but bottom there is, touched, up comes his
bucket, down plunges mine, you took it

I spoke of pleasure? Joy? ah, what are
these, who could question such necessities?

I meant maisterye, that luxury, he thought
she had thought, sighing, as he drew her under him,
    complying.

Dictation

At last the gods have left me
free to do
wherever I am moved,

am I forbidden? then
remember to forget,
if also only by

grave patterns
others wove in me —
abandoned

where I am
right, he is
wrong to me,

but in his own
right, right, as day
to me Pacific

over London lies
night, & rightly so,
what though I take it lightly?

Free to believe
whatever
will I will

I am, I
have that right
I've heard.

Please, Like Me

Strolling through the town, all the houses, quiet at this
    hour, the street
already hot, hold women. The leader
of our magazine crew knew how
to gain entrance by knowing that door
opening before the act, the door
opening. The woman, with him, his jacket
already hung on the back of a chair, his shirt coming off,
    crossed to the window
to pull the shade, making it
night. But in the morning, unknowing, despite the looks she
    gave him,
& me, watching, mentioned her husband, who handled such
    matters, her hands
at the necklace her throat was naked of —

Compliant women, my expression
insisted equally, Turn me away, & they would. A snapshot
one of them took, as I lugged up my arm
to knock, faded, falls from my wallet
as I count my take from last night, another subscription
    sold, working late, to think

great weight brought to bear on a door, that then
flies open at your first touch, so your momentum
pitches you sickeningly into the vacuum
cleaner, parked in the narrow hall, the muscles
involved with nothing to parry
ache, a nagging sense of something far
from being right. A wrench in the very
socket of the self, a disarming
tenderness, as if, on the instant, I stopped, now, knocked
here, went in, found
rose-lamps lit indistinctly for the sun that floods the room —

The brakes, the skid begun, surface
slick with the summer shower, he jammed, the chevvie's
tires, nothing to grip on, slid the four of us

within inches of abruption.
Welcome, & again, Welcome. Make yourself
to home. Drove nails into the plaster that wouldn't support
    even
a picture, hardly a heavy piece, chiaroscuro print
cut with a knife from a library book because I
against all claims of social conscience, against all readers
whose thighs tomorrow
would push against the metal crosspiece of the turnstile,
    wanted it.

The blood
floods the shaft, half moon, focus in an enormity of sky
extends by fractions limits
the blood continuously feeds, skin, sinew, ligaments
wherein, a heaviness of pleasure. Posit

night, & it is night, a white
flashlight conjures a white door, a red
calls forth a red, With which you can't come in, she shouts
but that's no use. I want
All*right*, you sonofabitch, even though the sentiment itself
be but a bluff, I'll call you,
But useless, again, if the man on the path
must tell her what to say. She switches on her porchlight
& the day goes, that kind of light by which

the face that passed, translucent skin, nose freckled at what
    bridge it had, the eyes
prominent enough so light could be seen to pass in profile,
    through the pupil
nonetheless left dark, but liquid dark, the bones of the cheek
    & chin
so clean, had had its demonstration. I see nothing

but where, the path winding, I'd cut across her yard,
    trampled, she says,
the flowerbed. I look
back at the earth packed hard in the footprints, & think

the hardiness of snowdrops, if snowdrops they are, for
    which she fears.
How difficult not to apologize, the door closing, the day
returned, to discover what did lie over that embankment,
    the manager
in his souped-up heap had as it were promised to reveal—

The paving's crazy, okay, & I'm clumsy. Maybe
this year, no snowdrops. There, on the morning sidewalk,
kids, they ride their tricycles but the wheels, was it the heat
presented it so, the wheels hold still, one fell
I stooped to set back on his feet, hoping his mother
behind a lace drape might be watching, his knee
is grazed, deep, I wait, but no blood—

A disconsolate salesman sat on a step opposite told me after,
after I'd come back out of the house, past midnight it must
    have been, the boy
eventually did bleed. A young man he was with his big
case of samples, shy glance of a blue that morning's hot sky
    had—
was most sincere, that desperate rhetoric, & fluttery
hands. Around her porch light
moths, you have to brush by
before properly inside the house.
The teeth, your teeth & hers
knock painfully together.

A Slot

Speak to the beautiful creature.
Tell her she is so beautiful.

Or how tired you've grown of dealing with her,
how, from the nothing left, you'd give her all.

Just Think

Suppose a screen
repeated every swollen move
a second after its enactment —

how would that feel,
reel upon reel
compelling as the notion of
your children growing older
when you stared at one just then,

that you're illuminated by
some mystery
almost infinitely
smaller than your self,
the square you
could never make it through
at the back of the theater.

A Final Mission

Whoever stood furthest up the trail was master
of the trail, which for the most part climbs
through a beautiful if crowded forest, though the final
four or five hundred yards rise
above the tree-line, across tricky scree, & end
at that peak which is also the scarp-edge, a steep
&, despite the rumors, inaccessible, drop
on one side, the shallow slope on the other, where the wood
grows, that is mainly conifers.
                                  To be master
meant, to gather all those things the ownership of which
proves masterhood, a tribute
all other travelers are bound to pay.
                                  Two friends
who thought to scorn such enchantments
were walking through this wood one day side by side,
they were talking, an old story begun
as they entered the shade, wherein the trees
addressed a pair of wanderers with promises of succour,
     when
first one friend then the other heard
the branches whisper, as if to himself alone, & suddenly

a woman, naked, broad-hipped & sloping of shoulder,
     stepped
out of a thicket, & beckoned.
                                  Now both these men
in flight from a band of relatives who
were pillaging their homesteads, hoped
in the remotest hollow of the forest to find
sanctuary in an abandoned mill of which they'd read

yet the sight of this creature
turned them, & they fell to arguing, which of them
first should address himself to her, who stood
expectantly by. They decided, finally, the softer
spoken should, he who had first heard the trees

murmur, his companion making a joke of it remarking Your
    mother
saw to it you were raised up with a due respect for
womanhood. No sooner however was this agreed upon than
    he,
this pleasant man, began to waver,
wondering whether the other might not be better for the job,
    & even
expressing doubt, that he himself had any
rights in this matter, Perhaps, he chuckled, I'm not
really here at all. He was pushed forward though
but when he approached the lady she told him,
she might only yield herself
to the master of the trail. The man considered
keeping this a secret, he could hurry on ahead
& leave his fellow to a futile wooing. No,
taken so, this opportunity would afford him no joy, he saw,
    the flowers
at his feet glazed mottled as tapestry at the mere thought

so he returned to his friend & together
they started to race up the trail. First one
then the other gained ground till very shortly both
lay grimy & soaked with sweat. This was on the near
bank of a deep creek, across which only a slim sapling
served for a bridge. The man who had addressed the lady
    lay
back & closed his eyes, he was seeing her beauty again, then
hearing a noise, sat up, & found his friend
on the far bank, had pitched the sapling into the creek
where it rode like a gigantic snake. There was nothing
for it but to swim, the current so strong
& hindered as he was by the young tree,
he could think it was actively
following, it took him
a good quarter of an hour.

                    Running on,
he became bewildered, the forest growth seemed to be rooms
filled with men and women, something small

34

clutched at him, asking he thought for help, maybe
he ran down the main street of his own village, smoke then
& not sweat stung his eyes to tears, & the music
he realized now had been with him all along, was folk
    tunes, he'd heard
sung about the kitchen, & danced to, Saturdays, the beat
his own heart, reaching the head of the forest

to see how the other had the lady by one hand

white it was as a tree where the bark is stripped back.
I will stop now, he said to himself, I will
lay myself down in this small bed & when I wake
a smell of pancakes & coffee cooking will be floating in the
    window
but he had forgotten to open it, to get the fresh air while he
    slept,
& getting out of the blankets he tripped, his foot
tangled in a branch a fallen hemlock farther on had laid
    across his path

so he summoned up what breath the altitude allowed, leapt
    forward, passing
around the couple, taking care not to
meet their eyes, & scrambled on until the peak was gained,
    where the trail
ended. He was so high
he could see not only the whole forest,
but beyond too, way down to the plain, where smoke
from the burning villages roiled
in a huge cloud, driven by a wind
which lifted the forest music into great chords of solemn
moment, & carried an odor like semen he remembered must
    be
from the soap-factory in his home-town, itself, then, ablaze.
Excited, he called down, that now the woman
should come up to him. Now

she appears to grow smaller with each step
although she all the while approaches her

master, who with bated
belly, waits, his pinions from his gleaming flanks
stir towards her, twenty yards away she is
tall as a five-year-old girl, till she climbs up his thighs
& unbuttoning him, thrusts in her legs
diminished to the size of testicles, & hangs
backwards, her toes hooked
in the asshole he by constricting can cause to raise
his darling, held rigid, till her sweet face reflects
that gleam the sun makes of his metallic fuselage

& together they move out over the forest
edge, where from a height of five hundred feet he can see
each husk of each ear on each blade of wild-oat grass
his friend & the lady in their brief possession or abandon
    had
pressed flat, despite the shadow
that he casts, by means of his appendage,
loving jelly down into, whereat the neighboring trees
his friend, who will not appear to accept such gifts, must
    have taken
shelter somewhere under, themselves take flight
—that the forest, whatever happens, persists
is foretold in the pitch
those screams assume from the shape of the falling stuff—
from the white-hot heart of the cones of flame
by which all is laid waste.

My Fault

You understood all about me & wouldn't
hear any different whatever the evidence adduced
against me, I loved you for that

if only that to myself I stayed so enigmatic, so
that I in my confusion sought you out —

&, apart from our arguments, that left me utterly
desolate, & you apparently
bewildered,
that soon passed, sooner for you
such was your love, happiness

was ours — I still see the cottage
with the cosy room, my study, with its roof
sloping either way down to
thigh-level, so only an infant could've stood
upright, & its one window where,
struggling to get my understanding clear, I'd stare

out through the blossoms I always remember as being there
although we spent two winters in it. . . .

To cease these preoccupations, crawling in
beside you, in the room opposite, & in your arms
find sleep, a heavenly relief

godknows — where god is
the margin where
otherwise I might've wandered alone, the name
given to all those
enigmas of disequilibrium summed
up for me in your laugh

remarkable in its assurance, if I was being stubborn
so sooner or later I could come around
to acknowledge my perversity
& you never bore me any grudge

that I could see, when gracious as that view
you opened up to me, who might show you who you were

so that we slept, you wouldn't take advantage of my rage
to treat me differently
so that I'd have to tear myself away from there.

Counted Blessings

Headlong means
heart leads, hands
insinuate, cupidinous
flies. The gamete
asks no unanswerable
questions. Papillae
a story of their own
for us to tell. As
the ovaries to pro
gesterone, so to
dirigibles, the fig.
Ichor! Fellatio. Sonar,
chiromancy, to open
that cactus. Labio
velars, night-blooming
cereus. They kiss
the glass bookcase.

In Time

At the last minute
it will come

too late to prevent the unfolding
begun long before its arrival—

As you're on your way out it'll fix you
so you will change your plans

to stay within its ambience
now that this place is

beginning to make such sense,
even though what now you've known

might reconcile you to departure,
the vulnerable one demands

that you survive, requires
all of your care,

yet don't you grasp, that it must go
on, twisted

past your recognition, if you
could be there, to witness—

what would your counsel anyway
have been, if time had granted—

for all your love
is the mystery, & strikes you dumb

explaining how to guard against
these gifts time rips from you.

After the Engraving

for Tom Clark

What I am fashioning
with my light chisel
is an amulet to hang
round my love's neck

against disaster
dwelling in the hollows
well below, a spell
to keep the evil there

where she will never let me go
to fetch one home, to petrify
& carve upon, so I am making-do
by cutting-up an earlier craftsman's

amulet, & yet
it sets her loveliness off wonderfully
now it is done, & seems to
keep its charge, despite

these haphazard city streets admit of no surprise
to violate her pose
under our cool skies
woven of rocks soil & stones.

Weight Less than the Shadow

We encounter in the lateral
tunnel at great depth, I wear
in my forehead a Davy lamp, newly acquired, the gift
in fact of a young lady, casts
an intense circle beyond whose rocky confines

blackness, nothing, your seamed
face as in a developing fluid coagulates, the lips
lift to tell me I have not yet
solved the riddle of the universe.

The bird in the cage I carry
has died, you point out. Misled,
I've gotten off the elevator at
the wrong level. You shrug
but cast the dies on my behalf. Back
they indicate, to the pit-head, collect
nothing from the company store, except —

I sank these shafts! Your fierce outburst, at last
to hear that voice — an obscene
gesture next, old man, brown shapes of continents
on the skin, over the excited hands, sarcastic,
This far down, we use
another kind of pickaxe — the right
hand, forefinger extended, lightly taps your temple, till

quickly, down to the pocket, still . . .
And what do you come up with but a two dollar bill?

I'm to buy a ball-point pen & five
blue (examination) booklets at the commissary, this is
becoming ridiculous, a dream, four of them
to wrap my lunchtime apples in, the fifth
turns into a bluebird for my cage.
I'll ride it out.
You pull your plastic goggles

42

down, over your eyes, & I
see, just as you'd turn away, my

self, indistinctly, reflecting.
The noon, leaving the "lift" (your term)
aches, blindingly. Some small
soft hand clasps mine, or a man's
hand merely does she grasp?

Maintaining she'll lead me
away from the pitfalls, she
takes me in a suspect tangent.
Dazzled still. My other senses would rescue me, my watch
beats, my heart
's an army on the march of ragged & conflicting voices
raised in a song they argue in the singing, is it
not my comrades changing shifts, that late already —

Globules of soil roll under my stumbling
progress, if that's the word. There,
she (you) says, she
laughs, dimly her face swims clear, There,

I bought your silly bird but
he wanted out, & so — the grilled
small gate hangs open. Next minute we hear
how good a cook she is. Next

you, old mole, working right through lunchbreak, under our
    feet, knock,
I mean, deeprooted trees vibrate about me.
Not Verk, you said, simply
Zuh tunnelss are unendting. How can I confront you, the
    cage

of an absconded trapeze artist, will you be angry? I won't
descend. Will you shrug merely? I won't
come again. She is leading me on, she laughs. I
won't budge. But the whistle
at the pit-head shrills

till everyone is in the evening elevator down, I'd slept,
dried spittle. But the whistle

—the naked lady has her gift, she hears it as music.
The coaldust on her sheets.
The mine I'd thought lay hidden, the fumes
however render a whole district, mine.
Her hard mattress. Motionless. The stars
are insatiable holes, we argue, I hold them
Davy lamps. The stars
are. The night is
cold, I slurred the word, is
coal, I said, & she heard, the blonde kiss holding, Gold.

A High Mass

At last I'm collected enough to let the ceremony commence,
my whole being shakes to an integral & simple beat begins
in one small muscle, five strings of fibers, as one
plucks the strings of its guitar, not the muscle wherefrom the
    clamorous
blood leaps, that loudspeaker, but maybe in my belly

while the cells of my body glisten, skin, sweat
it may be thought or the moistness of four thousand
excited eyes, my members
dance with one another, limberly swinging, never for long
    do they touch
but in relation to another writhe, in tangent to a dozen
    others, to the total

I, alone dancing, an oceanic joy I'm bathed in, so certain
particles of skin flake off, like a woman or a man go reeling
to a wall all out of breath, by such minute amounts my size
does vary, yet is exactly right, though there are those

older, they believe, who forget just how ancient is my kind,
    who can't
discern the Mediterranean in my demeanour, the Egypt
bulge of bicep & thigh, the way
hands pull on ropes to raise caked great black blocks of
    sound, or see
hair like feathers bringing the tribal invocation in

who sigh, in one hole in this hall
like a hole in a sieve, like a very small doorway
one of these heretics leans, stronger than these
strips of dead skin to be sure, all of a finger's height
he is, believing he's amputated, hoping to go it alone.

PART TWO
Choosing the Event

In His Image

"Having died
I was laid with eyes wide open in an open kind of grave
Tesselated marble, glazed
I gazed up at the sky
A stoned & Mayday gritty kind of sky

The camera stopped pretending to be me
to show I lay, all senses but this vision numb, in a wide
    screen
of sky & tile, to reveal the aqueduct
(disused I guess) that held me up

Down, down, a long way, to the ground, no
to the river" a voice said
"The better the life he lived
the higher they raised him from the waters"

The Arbitrators

Can I get it this once in my lifetime, now
I must get it immediately—

what *it* was
they let me know,

a question
followed hard by
a demand.

First

One aches to know
one fact as axiom
to act.

Despair
however one does, the word
depends upon another, is
désespoir, mere
lack of hope, & dies
with my belief.

So hope is first.
No, spoken first

against the
what I have to call the
silence, though a kind
a kind of
humming intervenes

of an instance as this evening
lying on
a bed I lack
energy to make,
to look
into the black
gathers at the ceiling
from a lamp I lack the energy
to break.

A Secret

Three times in the night I woke
blindly to write in three
phrases on a handy envelope

the secret
that is
the destiny of more than me
to crave
       to search
           to know

—when I woke for the final time I wouldn't look at it.
I decided to take it with me on my morning walk, tucked it
as an afterthought, into my hip pocket. I figured
I'd want someplace to stop, decode, & crow.

But it was a tangled day—that
let me, *led* me, to forget
& then I found it gone—

this is the secret
I am speaking of,
compassion made me wonder whether
I would tell you
but I can't,
as it appears,
any longer bear to
keep it
to my self.

The Accident

Up all night
thinking to write

a poem, now
at the door,

blue light! & a damp
mild breeze.

Let the news
paper lie

& stare. Unseen
by who? The white unchristened

ship leans into
a like blue.

All yours,
not the usual

when I forget
where the street leads

& think I recall.
Like nothing

but itself, the moment
nor the door

ever opened (by) me
before.

Sitting Across from the Mother

Sitting across from
the mother

nursing her baby, gazing
"vacantly" into space, I

see her as
another, a not

her, & desire (the naked
breast) leaps

instant as recognition
of the thing seen

stripped
of habit —

follows swiftly
tenderness (she is

not that other) only
as a known dress

falling all about her
& becoming

the two-in
one.

Ascribing a Motive

If I can fake
an ambiguous enough
sequence of events in
here, maybe they'll be drawn

far enough into the light
these windows let onto the yard
to show me what
was going on out there.

Eternal Image

The spider's legs
scrabbling on the glass
inside the jar

& the ticking of the kitchen clock

I can't show you the spider
except to say
it's bigger than I knew
spiders grew to be out here

& when I thought it'd escaped
the hair rose
over all of me
it was at least that huge.

The Future Is Our Mother

Constantly she gives us birth.
We read in where we've been
what we are constantly
about to be. In action
each is born anew
when the future is behind us.
And if it's all too much for one
then back into the womb one tries to go.

On a Photograph from Childhood:
Of My Mother, My Sister, & Me

Everything happens for the first time ever.
That's how we recognize it. When we do
that's why we smile like that
& how come I can say
that's what this picture's saying:
the Lord, they say, will know his own.

These dispositions of the dark & light
the mind needs for its ease.
What we saw then
we see now
except for her who held us
who has met it
yet dreams on with her arms around us
assured we'll be together
once again.

A Definition

If anyone speaks, it gets light

"I drink, I get high
to spite the dark"
among other things. Going for a drive, but, to
someplace.

Quick, I think, &, spark,

syllables ring
upon, in light, there is a blackness lying, a dying
fall, pupil, core, stalks
back into a brain.

A confusion of hungers
the tongue proves, selecting thoughts from thought—

To speak about, formulate
what pleasurable terror's to be had from, hid in
such a landscape, turns

a bottle upside down, the hand
hard, its heel struck against the bottom, not a drop
left. Pleasure in the company is taken

into a trapped place, the car
climbing into low hills, many bends obscure, when
        somebody up from the throat makes
sound, spiteful, obscene.
It
refuses
to grow dark.

What Friends

What friends came to be my comfort?
I cannot name them all — Red,
Blue, Yellow . . .

Yet remembering you
I turned them away.
You would have known how to use them.

Blue, Red, Yellow

Blue, red, & yellow
thread within, without
blue, red, yellow &
some further kinds
of happening that color,
here, is to be token of.

Blue can discover
blue beyond itself
& bluely testify
against the redness in the head
such blue
truth exists, & soon
perhaps comes proof,
as something built of blue
begins to function.

What yellow madness, to insist
all's blue, or nothing is.

The words are brown.
They shift from bluish
through yellowish to
reddish, brown. What if an unnamed color

wants voice, what choice
among the primaries
that the brain is
fixed within —

A Mystery

As for my face
I am less certain
when I see with what
assurance you wear yours —

a woman
inviting me to enter
the realm of such
appraisal as you

offer words, the food & implements —
don't you sense
in this instant clarity I've gone
beyond, your furniture

become a bunker? no,
an occult nest
wherein the worst
monster I can conjure

folds where I sit
into a mass less shapeless
than a ball, for all
your judgment rolls

impotently off
my surfaces (I am
another kind), as it
would do, were I

able to be sure
my singular
being has beauty fed
by nothing more or less

than my steady
articulation of that fact,

a truth
endlessly hazardous,

even as yours
in yours
that shows me otherwise —
yet I am sure in that.

A Defect

The doctors doubted any cause
since birth or even conception

but he finds a way to suffer it.
Couldn't it have been something

I did? Long ago, some blow struck
for meaning.

Choosing the Event

They want to be remembered for what they have done
as I was taught too, although we continue to live
but if you're an unlucky gambler
do you have to be a poor loser also? Why not
—"the bitterest men in the world—
they laid it on the line—
& nobody cares any more." Some D-Day hero
in the Chronicle because he had to
endure what he trusts never to endure again
doesn't want to forget the suffering
or does?

            Or say you were on a rooftop
& in agony lost all you had
to lose—let's say because you wanted to be free—how,
if you're not past feeling now, do you feel
when others take upon themselves to speak
for you, interpreters
who negotiate your silence?
If they're mistaken, how to let them know—
if you are gone, who do they speak for
but themselves, thinking what they want
was what you wanted too
&/or are wanting still, freedom

to think for yourself & constantly
to change your mind, from any man's
over you, any man that enigmatic
we have to appeal to him
in phrases the helplessness of which that act reveals,
so that when your back is shot or
turned, the man can plant equipment in your car
making it all all right in San Fernando
while the living speak of death in vain, in vain.

Why I Went There

Why I went there I don't know.
Dropping in unexpectedly like I did
where I've never felt sure of my welcome.
And an unfamiliar crowd — though I could be certain of two
who would put me down, if the opportunity afforded.

but that Barrie should be there, his hand extended
& that in that greeting, ten years fell away
& that, though friends had told me, he'd grown fat
I was disappointed in that — prospering,
the guest of honor of a famous editor yet.

They all went on to another party leaving me
to look for you, way down on Grove, night
having come uncommonly early
& you were way past the time we had agreed on

to meet, in this district where just last week,
two acquaintances got beaten up

— this is all pretty straightforward, *you* stayed vague
as actual person, but the charge of feeling
allowable only when dreaming? like the turning of a head
once seen, giving all a commonality of meaning
— *you* were this composition of those loves, become my son
& the location of his kindergarden
& the fact of my separation from his mother
that keeps me here, where I can't find a job

accounts for the buried resentment, the barrier
— the heaviness man is. But that,
suspecting Barrie would now be alone
with that editor in his apartment
where the closest phone was, I might use
to call the cops, asking for news of you

& that, when I forced myself to go there,
this party was going on, & I forgot to phone

this is the essence, where mine
& the general nightmare mesh.

So

So these were kittens, this the kittens'
basket was their bed, their
home, these eyes
looking back at his,
their eyes. The vowels
mesh with the consonants

& on that screen the words
form, *if I can concentrate* —
a pining, as if one might
crawl in among their number

to partake. But the assurance,
reprimanding one for his mistake,
is that voice I longed to join
mine to, that resonates

demanding that I get it right —
I hear it echo even in the slyness
when I disobey yet try
pretending to be good
as the iamb haunts these signs of feeling
I'd be mine: Write

how it is meant —
how are the kittens
meant to be, stripes
I remember, but that's a beating too, & rank — dapplings
as a general notion you
should see — he took the snapshot
fixing one instant

or my mother did, that, linked
making one time, moves
me, with these, back-in-on-out-to
where but here consorting with
memories I'm sorted by, that happiness
that slumped

him, that boy, against that door,
found in a litter, though we say
lost, of these concentrated joys —

when they told him, drowned,
what explanation had they offered —
the farmer couldn't see the use of them?

His misery I think was twisted through with wonder
drawing him to words like death or loss
asunder with fresh life —

then the resentment, that he hadn't been allowed to
witness what
he tried to figure out they hid with words —

Lots more cats come in a little while —

but never
these, not even
here, that's something else,

nor he
survive the general end to curl,
precisely so, in I again.

I Can't Read, & Here's a Book

I see him kneeling alone
in his room, sorting through what objects
choice & chance "conspire"

This is among the most poignant thoughts I know

The book I imagine is a 1945 edition
of Andersen's Fairy Tales
illustrated by Arthur Szyk

what makes me so uneasy, here, & why
am I driven to picture it?

How can I know
to what degree he is reflective,
what do I want of him. When he is
alone. When
I am alone. Thinking of him. When
I run out of
the particular kind of energy required
of me to be with him. & would sooner be alone
thinking, of him. However it hurts. Or soothes
what hurts. What displacing

makes him the book, while I am him?
How it feels, to be left out, closed out
of what all those others seem so vitally
to share. . . .

How can I be witness to a scene
that, were I there, would be different again

There's nothing here
I can't ignore, for
it's only in my brain.

3 Ways with the Same Sentence

I've been looking for perfection
but still am permitted to sleep
on our mattress with its
broken spring next to the
completion of your body.

Not so much lately since
circumstance has seduced me
away from the initial fervor but
in youth as with a mission
invited debauchery & remember
incidents of tenderness &
sanity that baffled me.

Godknows — god of my fathers
I have questioned all I could
yet still found means to live
when I woke up this morning nor
hold much hope things won't
once I am gone continue.

Made

Less wandering then than temporary places
laughter can afford, & kisses
& other making-do, while wanting
wanting

intermittently always
to reveal our real station in
this world
& to ourselves

& do we
shrink
from filling it

with this, & questions
similarly
formal.

Me Too

I did just what I wanted to —
dressed in my uniform
I wore, and
under orders once more.

Precept

I've helped you in the past
Go ahead, help me in the past again

Logical Conclusions

If you went over to some friends, a couple you know, say,
& knocked & knocked, & waited (the light was on), & then
knocked some more — & then
tried the door, so that it
opened, & you went in,
& found them sitting there. Would you want to stay?

If they leapt up & welcomed you, would you ever
trust them again?

I Read This Someplace

The lyre bird
amid the eucalyptus
listening for every sound he hears
to trip him into sound he makes.
He has no call or song
his own. He imitates. Each time
he utters something chances are
it is his soul that speaks.

Born Again

Let me be born again. Let me
literally be spirited
back within my mother who
equally miraculously
let be live as once she was.
Let me decide just where & when
& in what set of circumstances I
shall this time choose to enter.
Let me think.

Because

the garage hasn't any proper floor but earth
now turned to mud, we dug a shallow ditch
across the field that slopes down from the house.
Today the ducks drink from it.

Today I know one cause why men go to war.

Oh, the chores undone.

Log

Fire's here, that won't be forgotten.
Nor will light, & ways to shade it.
The fire too has a stony hearth
to keep it in its place, and keep us safe.
Chairs will not & nor will tables
fade from the mind, walls & roof make shelter
because of cold & wind.
Dispose them in what attitudes one will

if belief seduces you to show the way —
else nothing can appear
in this place that's not this house
where the intermittent ground-beat
of those flames & what they feed on
sounds like wind against an obstacle.

Beyond the Constellations
Here & Now

Those two lights
lower than the others
I know are houses
because the hill, by night
invisible, they stand on's
saving me from what I see.

An Esthetic

The FM undercurrent
as I'm in this place
alone without the strength
to joy in solitude

today, just then,
attending to an ad,
taken with the tone,
how he isn't able,

if he wants to sell,
to sound as though he
takes it seriously —
all such intentions these days

verge on this in language,
either we
have to laugh or
the propagandist does —

but once I found a letter
like from Whitman's God
dropped on the street
& spent an evening

figuring it out —
not to mention diaries
read illicitly, for instance
Leslie P's.

Outside

The fog so thick
that when I stepped outside
just now, the house-lights
threw my shadow, huge, against it—
I guess the Specter of the Brocken's
much the same.
                Condensing on the trees
it falls like rain,
the barren clay,
where I took such strolls last summer,
is thick these days, with grass.
What solitude

& silence, outside there—in quality
different from being in a forest, this is mainly
open range, but the solitude is common
to my thought. I thought

characters with mighty limbs,
furred, as cave-bears yes,
but more immediately
furred as trees with moss—

having believed—say, felt the force—
those tales of Bigfoot have,
among the redwoods, all alone
yet not, animals, perhaps inimical,
brush, furred, against the stiller
forms life also takes—

an intermediary
partaking of our, human, traits
yet of the terror also
that the forest holds, as one
faces him self in to it,

has its necessity—huge
as trees, that threaten us,

74

if such be felt. Some tales
will show them friendly,
children play with them,
they could, I know,
defend me. A certain logic

favors them, says this voice
I place within my head,
& logic,
          condensed
in my imagination.

I Know

I know we'll make love this Wednesday.
I know I've often been mistaken.
I know hope springs eternal but
forget how it goes on.

I know disappointment makes me bitter.
I know why love is said
to make the world go round.
I know other ways to say this.

I know there's no going back,
no other way to say this.
I know how we'll caress & this
is how I know.

Wisdom Knows

for David Weiner

Wisdom knows
its moon shines on
the topside of these clouds

Its light reveals apparent error,
telling us that, No, it's so,
on any night, someplace wisdom knows.

A Nest

The first nest
discovered in a hedge
containing eggs
was wonderful

way past the edges
that day made, for now
the marvel & the vision
together come once more

I see I saw what spoke
of shapes like it I held
within my self, & how
my joy would be material

of correspondent kind,
speech surrounded me from birth,
& the weaving of what came to hand
as mouth, was I

to be the center always
or some form
more knowable? I
was drawn on to discover

what drew wonder
from its contents that
grew wonderful so held,
such joy's its own reward

that has within its
dynamism the demand
to tell of it, & stand for
what it can't understand.

The Meaning Alters

The meaning alters
more swiftly than I follow
how I know. You dim

before my vision dims
or dim with it as I
dim, dim, the single clarity

you gave to see you in.
There is a nature we may trust
allegedly, beyond all doubt

these past two weeks the mist
that rises thickly from the ground
it hides, burns off by midday

allegorically, the fog within.
Must be a nature I can trust,
we did. We dimmed

swiftly, out of touch
of our desire. I must
trust my reading of my,

of our, of your desire.
More swiftly than I follow
how I know, trusting then,

grounded, meaning
grounded, this I know.
Imageless, the sounds

would fill with what, that fog
means ground I know, that
fog can ground that meaning

I took to know you in.
Swiftly, & dim, my clarity
is gone, it isn't she

I celebrate, if dimly,
swiftly, hurried her or me
out of our touch, the meaning

alters, our nature
can't be otherwise than you
I know, let you take the meaning

so my vision's flush
with its envisioning,
that had been our desire.

4 Pieces for 4 Voices Interrupting 1 for None

1

When I take a walk with you
I take several hundred steps

then fall flat on my face.
This once I'll tell you why.

I am trying to alarm you
because I want to harm you.

That clears up a part of it,
but part remains a mystery:

the way that I restrain myself
& how I know to come off it.

2

I am a student from Cambridge University,
you can tell a stranger

anything, that's why I love to travel.
Anonymity. Actually

I was working on a farm
having flunked 10th grade. He was

the owner of a restaurant.
And I believed him.

3

Something representing an intent
occurring where he reads it with

what one can call his paranoia
because he takes it to be true

infuses all behavior
— behavior all infuses

because he takes it to be true
what one can call his paranoia

occurring where he reads it with
something representing an intent.

4

Try as you might to hide it,
yours is a suspicious nature.

So we really had to work to set you up.
Lucky in love, lucky at cards, lucky

us to have at our disposal
all the secret agencies

of your experience — lucky
you, to have enjoyed so much.

But this is it. The way you knew
that it'd end. We're giving up.

The Objectionable

My Idea
had no room
for you
in it,

taking form
from Form I
had to act,
degenerate

perfection of
what's possible —
& room for you
describing it.

Continuous

Continuous
manifold, speech
is discrete.

Poems being speech
made real — or
if false, that also

must be real. Poems
being true,
true too what is,

that is
continuous. This
ceases, brings

its many intermittencies
to rest. The rest
is

diaries.

Credo

Art isn't the ultimate human act so for its sake I will
go blind & deaf & dumb, become a monster of denial.

Even Now

Where I grew up, imagine it's late summer, it can be
getting on for midnight & still light, & hot,
the day's heat hanging in the streets I'd go, this evening,
out into, to explore. Our family
had just moved to this district, so, this time
I speak of, I hadn't any friends
but wanted to go out as if I had —
better, this way, on my own, to go
wherever the mood took me, a friend
might be more trouble than I wanted.

But anyway, I hadn't one. And went,
promising, as I was made to, just for half-an-hour,
till bedtime. Bed would be a misery,
a suffocation, the sheets that strap you down,
the door kept closed to keep the light out
& their voices, that come in anyway,
though not so's you could understand.

I couldn't think of all of that. Not that,
having promised, I forgot. I let one street
lead to the next, but not so's I got lost.
I never could. I always had a picture,
the way I'd come, & how it led me back.
I looked into gardens, & in through lighted windows
at the strange order there, imagining
myself among those people & their furniture,
I might be one of them. I couldn't tell
how it was growing darker, my pupils
widening with the fading of the light.

I heard their voices, & saw that it was almost dark.
I was in a dead-end alley in back of a store.
The wall it ended in was brick, & high, & they
were walking up the street behind the wall.
My father's voice was angry, I could hear
she was worried, too. Any moment now
they'd turn the corner past the store & catch me.

As soon as they'd gone past the wall
I tried to climb it, but no luck.
To one side of the store, back the other way,
& jutting out over the alley, was a billboard
advertising what I can't now say. Up the scaffolding
I went & clung there, as their voices
& their footsteps turned the corner, passed the alley,
still I didn't move, & sure enough,
I heard them coming back, their voices & their steps
re-pass the wall, & fade into the night,
for it *was* night, as now I had to see.

If I only had a friend along, to help distract them,
&, if that didn't work, to blame it on.
Even now, I could run after them,
show them how I wasn't lost,
hope they'd be so glad of that, they'd not be angry. . . .
Even now, I could . . . I could persuade them
that it's not too late,
crying in the dark to melt their hearts,
or biting back the tears,
to show them how grownup I am.

An End

You found the thing
& it was hurt &
came easily into your hands.

Alone, you might've nurtured it —
but one among a group
you gave in to their demands,

& trod the life from it. A recognition —
what fear is here
I do not want to crush,

& do. You come to tell me
what's been done
to let me know to what group you belong

while seeming to remove yourself from it.
Sanctimonious
I shout. You come

replete with reasons why it had to be —
you've studied grownups.
But since you killed

what you are speaking of
it doesn't matter
what you say, I say.

My morning's wounded —
I wish that all of you had been
indifferent, & left it

say to fate. Or brought the thing
stupefied with hope
into our home

& all the trouble we'd've taken on

to no end probably
but to make fear our friend,

before we buried it.

Fresh from Sleep

Forgiveness — what'd she
mean?

I'd say this room's some 10 x 12 x 8.
960 cu. ft.
Just got up to spit, so I paced it:
12, x, 14? — can't be sure — the bed + desk come
between me & one wall, & the wall opposite's
broken by a projecting closet. As for the height,
I still have to *assume* it's 8 feet.

Never knew it could be this cold in L.A.

Do you think they'll be up soon.

I could use a cup of coffee —

Took the coverlet off the bed last night,
& hung it over the window
so's the next day, the light shouldn't wake me.
Woke about dawn, shivering.

What time is it.
5 cars have gone by already (quiet street).

Plenty to look at here —
obviously where they put the kids.
But I want to go for a walk, restless,
one window has a screen nailed over it,
the other, the one it'd be easier to go through,
onto the front porch, is painted shut.

Hill opposite — quite rustic, houses, shack-y,
"climbing" up it. Or I would. I can see what
looks like a chicken-shed — a poplar — 6 fir trees
along its ridge — 5 thin pylons with innumerable cables
(count 'em?) attached — a radio transmitter?
Can't hear a thing.

While I'm looking, two cars drive by. One a small
truck with mattress in back —
put me on it!

Three.

Going to be a hot day, if I'm any judge.

I used to play the guitar once.
I tried, anyway.
Guess I should've stuck with it.

Should I have read that poem —
the one about the man grunting during a previous
reading — so close to the beginning of
last night's reading.
I wouldn't read it at the afternoon reading.
Drinks, in between.

She looked like a nurse, by the shoes.
First pedestrian.
Waiting for the hospital bus, back in
North Battleford —
I *think* I know how it felt,
but if I recall the same time in another mood,
wonder.

Surprisingly few cars on the freeway between 5
-5:30 p.m., yesterday. S kept speculating
as to their whereabouts.
"The Martians have landed."

One
   of
     the
       kids
         just
           had
          a
            piss
           !

Could I tiptoe out without waking the others.
What about the dog.

Besides, I'm kind've enjoying this.

This is a really nice block —
I can see how one wouldn't think so,
living here.

Where's the smog.

None even in Pomona . . . A handsome lass, that,
said I reminded her of her first love,
"But don't worry — you've established your
own identity."

Difficult to know what to say, to that.

Who was that, her husband wanted to know.
So did I, & I don't even know her.

Car stopping — negress, if one can say so,
Afro-American? a lady with dark skin — black? —
just say, *a woman* — some loss of accuracy,
of actions upon any hearer's understanding —
in nurse's uniform — picks up two more —
for the seven o'clock shift? You mean I only got
five hours sleep?!

Too late now — two more cars drive by.

Three.

Think I'll get up & walk right out there
& boil some water.

*

20 *to* 7! how'm I going to get through the day.
Wait & see.

At least, got a spoon—I can eat my yoghurt.
Smells better than it tastes. Have I carried it
around too long.

The girl, 7, 8, was awake, gave a big smile as I
tiptoed past.

Birds, for hours,
Fly away!

I don't really want to go for a walk.
I want S & wife to wake up & talk to me.

Let's see—3 kids, all school-age—
she'll have to be up by 7:30.
I could go for a walk till then.

What shall I say when I come in.

Hello.

PART THREE
Watchers of the Skies

They Are Eyes

They arise
intent on us
& their intent's
that we do good,

thus, to this end,
by being small,
they make us spacious
so that we know scope,

& are circular & flat
to make us know
how round & tall we are,
like wells, we are to lean into

to drink, & dip up
water for our brothers
& our sisters too —
they shine

not alone to say
Let your gleam be revealed
but to remind us of the darkness
that defines them —

aren't they enormous also
to help us to imagine
ant or bee or
cell of our own body,

& to warn us
we can be mistaken,
& more than one can count
or even see, because

if a body lose
awareness of its weight
among the billions of its kind
its life will waste —

& they are blind
to remind us obtuse creatures
each is
singular,

& to insist, You must
use your mind to make believe
the stories of the real you tell
are true, & to that end

we constellate.

The Point

The point is not the point —
the hand that indicates,
attended to, is meaningless,
too familiar to engage —

the barn that's indicated
burns but what of that?
We know wood catches fire.
It's just sensational.

Someone is pointing at the flames —
attention has been caught,
desire ignites — we see ourselves
as someone points them out.

Still There

The night mysterious with heat.
Its sky huge now with stars.
The people sprawled in ragged groups

their voices quiet yet audible,
what do they say? These constellations
are indistinguishable from where we sit.

A slight wind murmurs in the cypresses
set there to turn it back.
The distances among the clusters

are wildoat grass the sun's rays slowly leave.
What do we know. It ceases,
others come to see as much as we.

Those stars are me,
these sounds. Tears blur
& bring them to a field of points.

Watchers of the Skies

So you think there may be something to astrology
That human life to some degree or other
Must be influenced by planets & by stars

Though not completely
A range remains
A range for human action originating in oneself

Inspired by others probably
In response to other humans I expect
One way or another

You think that force from outer space
To some extent determines human fate
And by studying the lore

By applying one's mind to the records
Human beings have been keeping down the years
Each in his own time & place   Own language

Each in the year that that recorder was alive
Moving among his or her own kind
One can read how forces such as these

Influence behavior
So that a system one believes in operates
Assuring us both by   & of   its constancy

It's an attractive proposition
Not easy to discount
One can laugh at it but will it go away

A system of belief that has persisted as it has
Why shouldn't there be something to it
The moon pulls at the oceans & the land

We know the sun is source of all
Our all   How like these are to a planet & a star
How small they are compared to most

Of course they're relatively close
Humans have imagined them as wife & husband
Sun & daughter   Relatively

Each is close to us as a husband or a wife
Relative to men & women who aren't cohabiting with one
Or won't   Or can't   Or haven't for a while

Desire can see the outlines of the furthest mountain
But love is blind
One sees the Earth with fresh eyes from the moon

Why couldn't there be something to it
Perhaps it isn't true   It's valid though
Given the initial premise

Given that some heavenly body
Apparently remote
Could in a sense be thought to show an interest

Who wouldn't fall to plotting
Become familiar with its course
Its customary haunts   Already in its power

Once upon a time   In fact
Once upon a New Years Eve   The eve of 1800
Piazzi saw a star   It was quite small

Not catalogued   His heart leapt up
In the constellation Taurus
He called it Ceres

Though it was the first
Olbers took the next step
Using the ephemeris of Gauss

On March 28 1802   Not too far from Ceres
In his line of sight
A second planet in the gap

The so-called gap
Between Jupiter & Mars
Olbers wrote to Bode

Did Pallas & Ceres always travel in their current orbits
In peaceful proximation
Or are both debris of a former & a larger planet

Which exploded   Huth
Thought not   His mind was quite made up
Maybe he was right   I can't decide

These tiny planets are as old as all the others
The matter they are formed of
Coagulated   Forming many such small spheres

Not much time passed   Relatively speaking
Before astronomers began to tire of their profusion
Said one who has remained anonymous

Nonetheless we know his thoughts on this
One planetoid was a sensation
A dozen fine

Fifty were still interesting
Today I call them Vermin of the skies
Their number now is estimated to be 30,000

Or more than 30,000
We do not find them mentioned
In the ancients   Their lore doesn't exist

Except in recent books
Take Hermes for example
Astronomers could not give absolute assurance

That a body such as Hermes might not run into the Earth
In December 1937 Hermes passed the Earth
At a distance somewhat under 500,000 miles

This was not the closest that it could have come
It could have come as close as 220,000
Closer than the moon

With what anguish many must have waited
In Hell nor were they out of it
Until the future came to pass   And Hermes guided them

Are they to blame   It weighs 3000 million tons
Tiny for a planetoid   But many times the mass
Of the object which caused the mile-wide impact crater

Out in Arizona
What object   That object whose impact on what's known
    as Arizona
That crater tells us of

How to re-write the lore of planetary influence
Now that the planetoids are here to stay
And always were

Since at least 100 million years ago
About the time that flowers appeared on Earth
Flowers   Which Darwin called an abominable mystery

They spread so fast
Appeared so suddenly
Like the human beings their appearance is associated with

No doubt these asteroids or planetoids
Shed their rays upon our Earth
Exerted & exert their subtle influences

Hundreds of astronomers will testify to this
Since 1800
To their influence on human actions

Thought is action of a sort
And speech   Sad not to have a tape
An interview with Shakespeare   Dante

Reading in Italian
Thought that doesn't come to action though   Beyond its
    brain
Does it leave a trace

Fine indentations on the brainpan possibly
On cerebella long returned to earth
Such is our lot   We come back on earth

Writing is an act
Writing makes a kind of record
The records our astrology is founded on

These are written records in the main
Imperfect though
They leave a gap unfilled

The story of the planetoids
Of their effect on our behavior
This gap makes a kind of crater

What thoughts belong to them
Perhaps a pattern will appear
This present writing springs from them

But can influence be willed
It's more a matter of what dreams have they inspired
Since the explosion

The explosions   Hirayama
Thought there'd been not one but five
Each causing what already had been called a family

Because its members moved in similar orbits
Perhaps a complex of such patterns might be traced
Maybe direct examination of a planetoid

Will provide a clue   Eros
Is most likely Willy Ley believes
His book   Watchers of the Skies

Is cited here   He means astronomers
But each of us looks up from time to time
Struck with the beauty   Our souls are amplified

It's hard to stop
Harder to bear sometimes
And then this faculty can rescue us

And take us to its heavens
At times the stars   Venus   Mars   gleam through
At times shine on a pattern

Perhaps the truth that they appear to point to
Is recorded by the watchers
Of the postures of the watchers of the skies

Next Love

The heat put it in my mind
so when I saw that glow
on the horizon eastward, growing
while I watched, the prairie
all around me dry, ready for fire

my excitement told me
this was what I saw, burning
everywhere, fixed
by the wonder for five minutes
when I thought about it later, when I thought
to run back to the house & let them know

there was something someone ought to cope with,
somehow. Before I could the flickering
I'd read out of the wavering
as flame, congealed

till what was then revealed
as a huge moon, began its rise
to be a second marvel, a moon that large & orange,
complete,
            contained —

then the familiar diminishment & paling as it rode
higher, that ache
asking some participation that its shape
refuses, a lonely
circle, where the end begins.

Credences of Winter

The season has us by the throat.

This must at last be real.

Winter, now the bitter truth
drives into mouth & eye
and shrinks both to mean slits.

I mean to let my coat be turned
to winter, to vanish into it.

I mean to fly south out of it,
south of all envy of my memory & wings.

I mean to get up on my hind legs
on these drifts, to strip the trees
next summer won't be able to disguise.

I mean to find another route,
to sail straight for it as if death
didn't mean the end, for those who follow.

I mean a house of ice
heated with the blood & breath of friends,
lit with the tales we tell of enemies,
of other nights, of hunger, that will end.

I mean less than may appear
to the one who traces back the turnings of my spoor
that led him to my fateful corpse.
The drifting whiteness blinded me.

I mean to burrow under it & sleep.
Who can imagine any other way.

I mean to crawl into this nest I built
of twigs the summer grew
and live on what I somehow knew in fall

to tuck away, & trust
winter told me to, & said enough.

I sang above the muskeg of the summer,
I mean to die.

I mean to live in snow,
to heat myself with ice, to eat
nothing but such fire,
to sleep wrapped only in the blizzard.

My word must be the last.

How else shall I find peace
if winter shaped my soul.

Seeing That You Asked

In this world there's a secret
& it belongs to me, to me
& to someone who lives in here with me.

When my brother dreams
he shivers. Instead of night
he sees these things.
When he takes a walk & sees something
it makes marks on his forehead
in small drops of blood.

A dream's when you see people.

The dream is in the smoke.
When you wake up
it's right in front of you.

The light makes dreams.
Dreams come to pay us back
& wake us up.

If you dream you're dressed
you see a picture.
As long as there's a picture in the room
I can never be alone.
Statues & pictures aren't alive.
They can only think & see.

The wind makes the grass move
& you see it move.
That is thinking.

When you can't remember something
then you think.

A horse thinks with its ears.
A curious thought came into my head:
I must give up my horse

to make my mother better.
It was made of wood, with real hair.

Could this chair have been called "Stuhl"?
Yes, that is a word in German.
Who gave things German names?
God, & the Germans.

A dog knows its name
but does a fish? It should,
if we know we belong, why shouldn't fish.

The name of the moon
isn't in the moon.
The sun's name's in the voice
that says it.

The clouds' name
is in the clouds
because they're gray.

As for the pencil,
it's printed on its side.

By Night

A man sits at his kitchen table.
It was dark and cold as this
before ever there were human beings.
In this large household he's a member of

the heat's been turned down and all the lights
but one, turned out. The people, so-called, turn
one to the other, huddled, mammals, into sleep.
Or turn to coupling now.

There comes a moaning through the walls.
The dog barks sharply, twice,
and the hackles rise on his master's neck.
Outside the window, only the stable stars.

He tells himself, No rules obtain,
but his household is under the rule of night.
A sleepwalking child would terrify this man.
He scratches at a pad in front of him

and tells himself, This is for tomorrow.
But he doesn't want to sleep. To dream
something left undone, back when, it ought to be
done once again, all combinations tried,

way back, when he was still asleep.
He discovers he's staring at the drawer,
the one where the knives are kept shut up.
There came a moaning through the walls back then.

Tomorrow will call it a freak storm.
He gives names to all the knives,
Tomorrow, Friend, Wife, Lover, Child.
He wants to sleep more deeply than they do,

a dreamless sleep. He scratches at his pad.
He draws the kitchen drawer, he draws it

open, he draws the knives in order,
sleeping there side by side. He draws

on, he draws the monster from the dreaming all
about this table where he sits. He starts
to draw the monster with a knife
but finds the light's too bright

and stops to turn it out. The night
comes through the walls,
the table turns into a wall.
He must not do as night dictates,

no, he must do as night dictates.
He feels about him for his pad.
He names one knife, I am, with what might be
another knife he writes, I am

to make the sun rise. Who are you?
Thin light begins to fix things outside
and then in. The dog looks up and grins.
The people, one by one, so dear,

appear. Gradually, their talk begins:
what's to be done in this day newly come.
They resist him when he asks them for their dreams.
And now the news comes on.

Old Fashioned Poem about God

I would acknowledge
the immense force
as the objective

for the lovers
hand in hand
vanish in that wave.

Ultimately, we are I,
the world's
perfect reflection.

How else should I
gain import?
And these insistencies

on the subjective
betray their panic,
trivially.

We live belonging.
But not to you,
or you. To God,

the vision of the whole,
this world has come
to shatter us.

More
Some / Dicta of William Blake

The authors are in the alphabet.

Print's in love with speech.

Folly runs out of time; wisdom's spaced.

Your reason rises, a shadowy horror, from the opened page.

Print organizes things for ever.

The library groans aloud at the birth of another subscriber.

Our bones will be ringed round with nets of iron.

The dead resemble ourselves : they had literate friends.

The order of words completes a circuit.

Time is turned into space.

There is no revision in the grave.

Frozen laughter coruscates in the moonlight of the eye.

The sun is as numerous as the optic nerve.

Space is a bruise inflicted by the Hammers of Los.

Texts cast long shadows to conceal the fugitive.

This sleep you would succumb to is called death it says
    here.

A letter is never a mental thing alone.

Lambs live a long time in our recipes.

Terror is mostly error; pi precedes it, why succeeds it.

Time — a bad workman but an undeniable monopolist.

The alphabet is happy to compose the book of love.

By Visible Truth We Mean the Apprehension of the Absolute Condition of Present Things

The kind of prose anybody can read. One Saturday night after the poetry-reading we went to a cafe to discuss it. Syntax like a clear window giving onto reality framed anew. Actually we went to a streetcorner near to 3 different cafes & discussed which of them would be best. How I saw it — I stake my life on such assumptions — shows me the way. None of them had room enough to accommodate everyone who needed to be there if no-one was to be left out. One leads instanter to the next, no matter I had those percepts. Driving home, later, we saw a remarkable sight: one car had to stop suddenly because of something we couldn't see that was happening ahead of it; & the car immediately behind the first car, had to jam its brakes to avoid a rear-ender. Painful, this disposition of each necessary element, as if a lawyer wrote it. Now the driver of the second car begins to blare his horn & one of its passengers even squeezes out of his door & brandishes his fist at the offender. We are reminded once again that justice is a passion. Even the interruptions lend it authenticity. The first car, now able to move ahead, did, the second car with a squeal of the tires in hot pursuit. And then it was we noticed that the second car was driving with its lights off. And thus we hold there are times when we can bear witness to the present condition of absolute things.

The Cause

I am the cock
to make the sun rise in you.

What is this gang of physicists
you keep back of the set.

Who are these insurance agents
forecasting your weather.

I am a fairminded person,
albeit male, who tolerates them all.

Here is the inevitable postcard,
sunset over Popocatepetl.

PART FOUR
The Art of Capitalism

The Art of Capitalism

I heard of this woman who loved to eat oranges.

Hey, a friend said to her, You should go see this movie
at the International Film Festival. It's just this woman
eating an orange for fifteen minutes in close-up.

So go she did.

Two weeks later, her husband finally notices something's
amiss with her. You've been pretty much depressed and off
your feed, he says. Why not eat an orange? I can eat an
orange better than the woman in that movie, she tells him.
I'm damned if I can see why I should have to eat oranges
and not get paid for it.

Ownership

You own me. Black light bores out of me. In
every direction, blocked. Each outrage you
have taken & transmuted to another failed
experiment in the evolution of your creature, me.
You win. Here is your prize: this shell that if
you only wish commemorates what took away our
breath: the winged thing I must be, & you have
lost.

After Brecht

Be thankful it's this dark.
Nobody knows what you're up to.
What if they did —
who's to say it's wrong?

Anything we want to do,
as long as we can find the energy,
we do it. That's how come
it's getting darker all the time.

What if some dark night
they do you in. No last moments
marred by the injustice of it all.
I don't know who to thank.

Objectively

a loudspeaker
mimicking loud

speakers speaks
the mind

licking the
popsicle

frozen of
itself

& isn't
sure

it likes its
taste.

Present Correct

Condition Absolute
obtains. No other candle
feeds my flame.
From here on in,
you gotta stop me,
I'm coming through unless.
This is *my* morality.
I offer what you want —
or the infinite advantage
of the wronged.

Person

I want to lie in the greasewood
with a rifle & pick off
strangers that pass in cars.
Who knows me, really.
It's all an act. But secretly
someone is alive in here,
someone I want you to meet.

In an Orchard, in America, in August

Let this be
the story of the core.
The part that's thrown away,
that can't be used.
That can't speak for itself,

so it must be told
through the flesh,
the sweet, the reasonable
medium, the flesh
that proves its core.

You hunger, you thirst,
yet you walk in an orchard
in August, a hundred
invitations crowd in on you,
one comes to hand, to mouth

and flesh assuages
flesh. The core
you fling away,
petulant, you bit into
an aftertaste that spoils

your meal, but
never mind, you're fed.
The core falls somewhere
and persists, the seeds
ensure this story

shall be told again:
in an orchard in August
you hunger, you thirst
for the story —
how the core depends

exactly underneath
the stalk, the line

of life, the flesh
swells out from it, as if
protective, cushioning

the life within.
Such russet skin!
Such placid swelling to
a form this apprehensible
you'd think it grew to

fit the hand, as at
a god's command.
Truly, we are blessed.
Truly, life knows best
just what it is about.

What abundance! Why not
that one, and not this —
why not both, or more —
you worked this orchard,
here, take your reward —

sweet reasoning indeed.
Life must go on.
Haven't you seen someone
eat one core and all,
and shuddered? The worm

is found most often there,
laid in the blossom
that will become the heart,
and burrows outwards,
if less often, to the edge:

these small dark marks
remind you. But
you're prepared,
take your knife
and cut that portion out.

Animate life has
preceded you, and you,
you will not eat it,
understandably.
It has destroyed the core,

the story of the core
also, is riddled with it.
Simpler to say, it spoils the taste.
Settle for what can be saved.
The core, you throw away.

Back to A's Place

After the reading we went back to A's place
where I spoke with a lot of poets
though by no means all those present, & ended up
downstairs in front of the tv with some more.

The show was for the silver anniversary,
it opened with a still
over which the camera panned
of the completely ruined city,
then zeroed in on that dome
the eye of the blast left intact. Slowly

it drew back to disclose a city
three times as big as the one in our name
murdered, & rebuilt,
as this second still showed,
entirely, save for that infuriating dome.

The Romance of the Automobile

It's dark. But there's a moon. You're lonely.
You've got me. You can't stay where you are.
You don't give me a thought, & climb inside,
turn me on, & off we go,
me all around you, moving you
while you sit still, up & down
the ground I keep you lifted from,
across the distance that your friends call you.

Though I can't see
with these things much like eyes
I let you find the way.
Let you see what you might hit & miss.
Let you feel you're in control.
Let you make me go so fast
you can't control me quite as well,
or maybe not at all.
So I get you where you go.

And if it's where you planned,
I've sheltered you from what came down,
proved useful, helped save a life maybe,
unless someone like you got in our way.

You've felt a strength, obeying me
while free to think of things along the way.
An irritation or anxiety,
if something's wrong with me,
that is, if I need fixing.

And here we are. You can get out,
and stretch, as though to throw me off,
as though I were around you, yet
I'm evidently not. You've turned me off,
locked me up, pocketed the key
and left me in the dark.
You've got me where you want me.
As if I were a car.

The Realist Surrenders Her Secret

Running my thumb over your face —
the colors are so delicate there,
they will be sought
then, found, we will attempt
to paint with them,
to make them be your face.

The Imagist Seizes His Opportunity

Driftwood, constancy.
How you withstand this sand,
although it bury you.

I should like to see the storm
that moves you on.
Hard to imagine you

never felt desire,
weathered limb.
There are stout-hearted trees.

You too speak my shame.
As this hand moves over you,
weighing your disappearance.

All That Remains of a Poem by Helmut Maria Solk

for Georg Gugelberger

She got a Mother's Cross
when her fifth was born
(quite a coincidence:
he died aged five months).

Instead of Heil Hitler she said Hello and So long.

In 1943 her husband was made special forces leader.
In 1944 her block was leveled.
Her neighbor took a board and wrote
Alles im Arsch! Ich geh bei Lotten
and stuck it in the brickpile.

One day at 5 o'clock the Frauenschaft
congratulated her
on the soldier's deaths of her three sons.

Five weeks later it was her husband's turn—
Ukrainian peasants
and quick surprise.
She went to Lotte.

During an air-raid she gave herself to her protector.
After five hours
and all those years
her longed-for orgasm
and countless tears.

Her daughter's into monuments.

Not Guilty

So that's your concern at this
script conference —

who pays the tuition,
who wins the prizes for poetry together

with the risibility of his intention,
the old movies that creep

whispering into your cot
like a not

so innocent
sister.

Soul Mates

The plague had been upon the land before he arrived but he had
to be responsible for it. He plucked out both his eyes. Four more
grew in his head & his responsibility doubled. He grew twice as
lonely & his despair led him to tear off both ears. Now he would
not have to attend to their accusations. But the expected hap-
pened & rather than speak of that he tore out his tongue. But
there were already more than enough mouths to be fed. He
became a member of a group dedicated to feeding them & im-
mediately the number of groups dedicated to starving them
doubled. He dug a hole thinking to pull it in after him but some-
one up & died in the one next to it & he lost his grip. He might
as well wish upon a star at this point to get him out, but which
one? In the morning his arms were discovered frozen in the at-
titudes of prayers. The suns rose, the arms thawed & fell off.
Now he had four & using two to hold his head, he cut it off with
the other two. He would never be alone again. He was terrified
the other head already had the plague, & that was how this
thought got into whichever was his. Whichever was his. He had
to be responsible for it. The plague had been upon the land before
he arrived.

Calm as the Night

the surcease of decision.
No memory without
the desire to remember.

No soon or never,
night's day.
No persons of no drama,
people? pah.
Monads with a scene to make

slick back their hair & pantomime
another time to make one,
disclosing the impossible.

No nature but a history,
no history but one can be
rewritten. All longing
gone. What I imitate
I am. I ought to be

abolished.

For San Antonio Estero

Such scenery wasn't always thought appealing. They found it lovely because it looked like pictures they had been told were so? As for the exercise, that could be had on any city block. The developers had already blazed a road over the hills to this valley. How lone it was, the estuary birds & a few sheep the only moving things beside themselves. It spoke to his soul. When would his soul fill up with houses, & catch up with the world he was born into? He watched the contractor's truck moving down the dirt road across the river. He hated whatever was driving it. He wanted the whole earth to return to the condition of this valley. His soul *was* filled with vast tracts of houses & demanded purgation. He too lived in a house, a hateful thing upon the grandeur of the earth's aloneness — a lonesome creature grand in its self-loathing, craving release to some simpler time, when emptiness was to be filled, not treasured as a no-man's-land to keep anguish homeless. Perhaps only the vastness of the prospect encouraged such abstraction. If he looked in front of him, climbing, he saw only innumerable blades of grass & a lot of grasshoppers.

The Art of Capitalism (somewhat later)

I heard of this man who liked to eat oranges.

Hey, a friend said to him, You should go see this movie
at the International Film Festival. It's just this man
eating an orange for fifteen minutes in close-up.

That's very unexpected, he said, I think I'll see it.

So see it he did.

Two days later, his wife notices something's troubling
him. You've been kind of quiet lately, she says. Would
you like me to get you an orange? Then we maybe could
talk. I can eat an orange better than that guy in the
movie, he yells. I'm damned if I can see why I should
have to eat oranges and not get paid more for it than he
probably got.

Rumor

A head, small for its weight
& with the tongue
uncomfortably apparent

was borne by where we stood
in a large green pick-up
with a german shepherd

(large also) barking in
some uncanny rhythm
we could not decode.

The nearest phone,
to our astonishment,
was functioning.

Persistent attempts
notwithstanding, nothing
more closely resembling

the decapitated body
implicated has turned up
than a single boot

of the kind favored among hikers
at the bottom of a duckpond
close by the phonebooth

with several small dark
stains discernible & most
obvious of all, a missing lace

much like the lace
we noticed you were wearing
yesterday although it actually

wasn't us but a stranger
with an interesting lisp
who saw the head.

Tall Portrait (2 or 3 storeys) of M.P. as D.B.

prespecular / crepuscular / spectacular

*

We are marching to Aporia

We're rolling some stones down to Rio
Nido, or rowing them, and I say
Isn't that a noted theorist

in his far from radical shirtsleeves

And I say, My quotidian acts
can never quite account for my art.
Then someone says, Here is *le mot juste*

and there is the text, for which I care

nothing, or which we are carefully
noting. Now one of us who was born
in Manhattan or from foreign parts

to emigrate or immigrate when

he was three or seven, projects a
bemusement over what it means to
be a man. Clad in an immense white

suit, shoulders nearly double the width

of his slender frame, possibly just
for fun, perhaps a critique of his
audience for empowering seeming

over reality (to which end

such stage clothing was put by Cocteau
and Picasso), his hair slicked straight back
like a 20's matinee idol

or to evoke an 80's mutant,

he demonstrates a repertoire of
electro-shock gestures and turkey-
neck tics as he intervenes against

his art on its behalf. Early in

the 70's, he affiliated
with conceptual minimalist
art then flourishing in the SoHo

district, where he mounted a number

of performances that teetered so
precariously between satire
and whimsicality, audiences

often failed to perceive their humor.

He once shaved off his beard to the tune
of "Pennies from Heaven" played on an
accordion while a woman who

stood center stage flashed cue cards bearing

Russian words. But soon a newer sound
began to crystallize inside his
head: funk rhythms fusing with DB's

own cerebral reinvention of

60's soul. With the group "Talking Heads"
he released an album which garnered
panegyrics from the elite rock

intelligentsia who welcomed

its rigorous structuralism.
This was shortly followed by *More Songs
About Buildings and Food*, and then by

Fear of Music. Lambasted for its

formalism, the group found stalwart
defenders, the *New York Times* among
these, to remark that they stripped music

of its false emotionality

to convey true feeling all the more
directly. His lyrics are simply
structured, in terse verbal units, like

dialog in a Beckett play. The

dissociated products of a
fractured sensibility, these works
pulse with urban tensions in fables

at once unsentimental and yet

chillingly evocative of states
of extreme neurasthenia, in
phrases that can seem *non sequiturs.*

Gaunt and ascetic-looking, Tony

Perkins shoulders tense and hunched, staring
straight ahead with Buster Keaton look,
he spins the car radio through the

latest hits by all his colleagues with

an impatient grimace, but Tina
Weymouth thinks he spends too much time with
persons with whom he has little in

common. DB has now achieved the

status of celebrity, so that
these words were for the most part taken
from articles in *Esquire, Rock &*

136

Roll Confidential, Ms, Rolling Stone,

and other journals enjoying a
large national readership, and from
the *Current Biographical Year-*

book. By his branchings-out into the

theater, movies and tv, he
threatens to break-up the group, or so
the latter fears. However, since their

Tom-Tom Club record outsold any

Talking Heads disc, Tina and hubby
Chris Franz have sensed some positive shift
in the balance of power. Today

he lives in a district of pricey

boutiques drawing hordes of tourists too
trendy for his taste. Singing is a
trick to get people to listen to

music for longer, DB writes, Than

they would ordinarily, so that,
given "We're on the Road to Nowhere,"
we might as well "come on inside" — words

sung to keep us listening to the exciting drums.

Able to Describe the Verses

(after Neruda)

Able to describe the verses more sad each night.

In the night like the two of them between my arms.
They kissed like tarantulas beneath an infinite sky.

She quizzed me, I quizzed her back.
As if I had a friend with big fizzy eyes.

Able to exactly as I said before.
Thinking that I can't go on. Feeling lost.

Ear to immensity's night, immense with her.
On the other hand my soul turns rocks into paste.

What does it matter my love can't guard its shame.
The night is starry & she isn't with me still.

So much for death. For song with its laws. For laws.
My soul is not contented with having lost her someplace.

As if she were here, I admire her hair suit.
My heart her hair suit, & she isn't in it.

The mismatched night blanks out the mismatched trees.
Our sisters, those who entice, the same backwards as
    forwards.

I don't know why, that's certain, perhaps I should ask her.
My voice grows furry as it blows about her idea.

The other. Be the Other. Come kiss me like before.
Her voice, her clear form. Her infinite pupils.

Why is night like the two of them between my arms:
my discontented soul with the beauty it has lost.

Why I don't know for sure, maybe we'll discuss some ways.
The short tan of love, the large tan of oblivion.

Although this sea is the ultimate sadness she can cause me,
&, as I told Sean, this is the ultimate paper boat I shall
    make her.

(TITLE DEFERRED)

Along with a lot of cheap copies of great Art they had Venus plastered to the wall behind a lacquer too thick for anybody's pencil to penetrate. But the cover itself would receive & preserve impressions & those who had been drawn to write on Beauty had plenty to say. It was mostly scornful. Despicably big drops of milk dripped from her tits. In mockery of Botticelli's tact, some jerkoff had added authentically leaden hair to her pubis. Pricks in both hands, etc. Some other artist of the immediate, fearful of passing through this place unnoticed, had paused long enough to remark that "Elitist" was the word uppermost in his thought.

Had these embellishers been driven to all this by her unattainability? Hardly. They'd have done it equally on the actual surface of the reproduction. They were as anxious to cover her up as her sister in real life, who holds a robe for her to don as soon as the Moment is done. It was her vacuous expression? Then that was their mistake, for this is not vacuity but absorption, neither self- nor selfless. Now he himself renewed his vow, to dig through all the crud they had laid between himself & her, to reach her one more time, to surrender to a music not at all his own. Someone was rattling the doorknob. He put his pencil back in his pants.

TITLE: In the Can at "The Grand Piano"

Doggone Real

*We have been earnest for so long, we have clean forgot
what nine-tenths of life is really like. —F. G. Hilde.*

1

Devrions-nous se lever et agir?
And each face searched his neighbor's.
We would speak better french
had we slept somewheres else than night-school.
However, the tiny wheels beneath our shoes
saw to it that we reached the High I.Q.
Convention, what a sight!
The part I personally enjoyed the most
entailed the ceremonial
burning of the toast,
and then the crowning of the smug young bastard
who would be drawn and quartered, sketched, turned blue,
re-designed, engraved and lacquered
this time next year. Our way lay West —
into the Desert of Fear.
Our two most favorite words are
oasis and mirage. They make us large,
stiff, swollen up and sort of purple
and ultimately, very wet,
enabling us to exit stage left humming.

2

In times to come, what will they make of this?
Our gestures indicated with one sweep
sun, moon, and elms, knitting, streets —
an undertaker sitting in the sun —
a bench beneath his buttocks —
oxcarts — the oxen's eyelashes, silver in the moon —
the vicar turning blue because he rides a bike —
they'll say we were all homesick, probably.
That's all they'll know, cried Bill,
he who left home at three, before the mast

crashed through the attic, making an orphan of his intuition.
And Aye! that's all
they'll know, chimed in Penelope,
her only childhood home a chest-of-drawers in Pireus.

3

Rare pleasures especially
delight us, or especially delight
us, says Epictetus, his head resting on my chest,
his left arm cuddling his sister,
and he persists in calling me long-distance
after midnight, whining that it's dawn
back east where he is, usually, and I tell him
it's been years since I saw snow
except in pictures. Only, tonight,
he's here. Snow was on our boots that day
we hit Destination-not-yet-city,
and pointed out the coil of rope hung on a barn
to one another, fiddling with our necks
and saying everything in quotes like actors will,
hoping that the show that evening prove
pleasing to these locals,
passing us by with heads downcast
and weather-bitten faces so averted
they had to have seen our likenesses on posters.

The snow that year was green.
The year was the year of the gunpowder odor,
usually accompanied by a picture of plums blossoming,
having some connection possibly
to all the dexedrine we did, were doing, and had done.
We got ourselves pitched into the slammer
and underwent all of the provincial tortures
of which the worst concerned a spider and attention-spans.
We expected to explode
and can't say what went wrong.

There was the person known to us as Earface,
Will ya lookit that, he'd always say.

Seen through bars,
streets with street-lighting arrangements were quite novel,
and whether in dwellings, furniture, the work of art, or tools,
or some bozo on his way to the P.O.
with a jiffy-envelope of snow
he meant to sell to his old grannie
doting on him back there in New Hampshire
flipping us the bird, we sought the new.
Flip me off would you?! Epictetus turned purple,
and his mouth grew wet,
and he shook his sister at the jerk,
—a rag-doll of strikingly original design,
its arms sewn to its ears
and knees bent the other way,
so it should never kneel.

4

Going to do the banking,
we had this much invested
we felt fat and sassy
and distinctly insecure,
why else strike up a conversation with the teller,
who to those among us sexually bent to fellas
was a fella, but to those
who want to know how it fell out with one of us called me,
was female and five foot three,
and by four-thirty would be free.

We kissed in a field of, frankly, fog,
each goose-bump on her thigh as high
as though I saw it in the mirror through binoculars.
In the back seat of the family confessional
she lowered onto and around our system of taxonomy
all she could spare of her political economy.
We agreed to meet again.

Going to do the banking,
sweat broke out upon our brow,
for as our balance grew, so grew our longing

to deposit, and as a consequence
we saw life in terms of the body-count between us and the
    window,
where, if we are ideas,
we can't be recognized unless
we stand in line, and, if we're something else,
smiling like it counts at every sign.

Broadside

Sell the key, change the face you chose
It was an earnest plea for the words
terrible and *desolate* to merge
to combine the discarded condom with the mercantile society
which your head contains, along with your hands
that want Ontario to be an oratorio:

your taste for auras and your appetite for money
finally make one another's acquaintance
as the note of reason is struck, stuck in the throat of
     necessity
and the sinuous line abolishes the page

The nude lump interrupts your dreams with fundamentals
"Promise to pay bearer 20 dollars in United States currency"
And that which you are able to alter
alters, and you are condemned to see.

Under Fluorescent Lights

(after Fantasia of the Unconscious)

Under fluorescent lights the voice is pitched high, starting from the larynx & resonating thinly in the maxillary sinoid cavities. By candlelight, the conditions otherwise unaltered, the voice is pitched considerably lower, rising from the diaphragm & resonating in the upper chest, the region of the great plexus of sympathetic feeling. The content of what's said is more kindly, painful to hear perhaps but spoken from the heart, sans the insincerities that so often shrill out of the cheeks & nose.

Sunlight, where the body of the speaker's exposed to its warmth, will locate the voice deep in the diaphragm, lulling the thoracic ganglion, focussing sensation in the solar plexus. An animal relaxation may inform such speech.

But today clouds beyond our volition make that impossible. However, anyone can light a candle or flick a switch, giving the other great truths their location.

Opening a Trap

We are taking it apart. Are you going to take a part. What part are you anyway & don't you have a way to go? To depart is to be in the way, in the way of being apart. Are we as partial to this plot as I am partial to you? Then, aren't we partners till death do us part? When the mortal part, that the plot parts to admit, departs, is there a part left? This is part of what we are going to take apart to give it a way. Part of our lot is art. If you are going to take up an art & give it a lot, it's got to be taken apart, that's part of the plot we take to be our lot. Without a common lot, what plot allots parts to each? We are not partial to a pilot whose plane is a plan he is not in. Part of the plot to be taken apart & allotted a way allows that as the waves part, love will depart the glottal depths & no longer be a presence apart, thickening the plot, blotting out such parts as you & I, in loyalty to the lottery, & the habit of commitment.

PART FIVE
Typicality Enthralls with its Particular Failure

If Wants to Be the Same

The mounting excitement
as we move
step by step
of difference
off the same

if wants to be the same

the same as *is*

Typicality Enthralls with its Particular Failures

Typicality enthralls with its particular failures. "My husband doesn't understand me at High and Academic — you'll come, can't you?" "Indefinitely." Ours is a century of manic specifiers who mistrust anything, so it's as though we knew one another already. Comparable plumbing. Incomparable plumbing. They hadn't realized their experience was general, before she imitated their behavior in the bathroom mirror. "Why (ah, why) do women have such smooth thighs . . . ?" "Because men like them that way." Into each life some rain must fall, but Teresa Brewer was merely singing what she'd been told to because I could be counted on to recognize it. Is that what makes the first person as singular as he is? The prepared person alone can be surprised into insatiable desire, for the blueprint cuts no lumber. There is the effect of superimposing a repetitive design, such as a grid, on the same or different design to produce a pattern distinct from its components. Are the performances, they wanted to know, what was predicted from the record? In this society, we shift social conflict to psychic problems that can thus be charged to individuals at 50 bucks an hour as private matters. But isn't a percentage of our wages intended to cover the case? It's not only embarrassing to be like a dumb Swede in an Ingmar Bergman movie, it's suicidal. Of course suicide can be the ethically correct choice. I think of him often.

Had he testified too personally (i.e., not personally enough) in his voluminous (i.e., not voluminous enough) ways, glued to the underside of all that he opposed? If mathematics is the analogy, what is this:

> Aimed at defining
> Simply transmit orders
> World go round
> Blow your wad
> Late at night
> On the level
> Times the mass
> The correct answer
> Heard while reading.

For those who learned to drink in the 50's, vibraphones will inevitably bring on a slight stagger. Down the steep steps he slipped with many abrasions, only to find the Club Serendipitée, where he caught some GREAT sounds being improv'd by those cats. Then this chick, see . . . but music must not identify its methods, a part of subjective reason, with the subject-matter, which is objective. There is nothing ambiguous about our *double entendres*. The poet, having no identity, is continually informing and filling some other body, and who isn't a poet, if by that this case means scorned, spurned, feverish, headed for death, name writ on water, way with words, incapable of not noticing all this and more upon occasion? Only the self-important have indecipherable signatures; that's what shy is. Sibyl, the psychological model (v. supra) for cutup, and not that this is; she clarifies universal tendency, stands for that freedom we seek from the rule of the monotone personality, and for the terror we fear from the trauma that fragments us. Viz: "I am my father on film desiring my body as a young man who must therefore be a young woman in love with my mother, herself admiring my young manhood in my father's frame, plus the two girls in the upper berth across the aisle who had a little mirror and pencil and paper, plus the grandmother chaperone in the lower berth plus the lady feel sad oracle experience received opinion hallmark conductor ejection." Everyone should think like this. Everyone does. Does what. Nods.

I am not the person to whom these things were done but those things were done and their memory is in this person as imagination. The crystal ball is one of us, you guess which. Who makes your decisions, if not for you?

Shrinking things making us feel bigger

The Cosmos, Psychiatry, Something
with sex written all under it. Etc., etc.

Comedian topples, finally, down manhole.
Audience swells with amusement, bursts

In two (applause). Two tiny tabs and he ex-
Claims at being everywhere almost at once.

Being. Everywhere. Fermis
Backfire: a Solitary Person

Standing for all of us
Between two double lines of cars,

(Standing for all of us also).

Time is attractive in a period of rapidly increasing wealth. We can hardly wait. You have to hear what we paid for this place and just guess what it's worth today. To impress the crowd's meanness upon himself, he envisaged the day when even the out-casts would be ready to advocate a well-ordered life, condemn libertinism, and reject everything except money. Easy for him to say. This first edition of Baudelaire set us back a pretty pen-ny. Why was an entire generation raised to despise money, and why did we have to be part of it? Its acquisition was supposed to breed callousness, but that was just our parents' opinion, and they're all dead now. But when money becomes the universal un-conscious (=ideology), we become, as always when what's unconscious is in control, inefficient as a species, firing whistle-blowers to perpetuate error nobody much cares about before the banks begin to fail. Then all hell breaks loose. The cliches smash through the backdrop, clanking. One minute, *Ordinary people* were reading *Sayonara* in the *ben-jo*. The next, *The Way of Zen* had led its *lotophagoi* to call the cops out. Clinamen's queer for exogamy, but right then a concluding ensemble, which serves as an epilogue, is frequently omitted.

The oppressive mis-use of the term *unique*, and let's include all valorization of the individual, with its particular voice, perpetua-tion of anachronistic hierarchies, cultivation of foible, stems from a prior suspicion, too feared to be acknowledged, that, by the terms of our society, namely, monetary worth, all are, however inequitably disposed along its curve, interchangeable units, defined as capable of causing amounts of currency to adhere to themselves. Sexual activity has become one of the chief mask-ing routines ideologically calculated to buy off any such awareness. Concurrently, an alternative system continues to operate, threatening even as it is threatened by the first one spoken

154

of here, whose units measure their abilities by different sets of criteria. But any one of us belongs to both systems. Is the pronoun *I* a healing declaration of self or the last refuge of a scoundrel? Write when you find out, or work.

Our frequencies

Always excepting time,
people the most commonly employed,
a little more than water,
a little more than words.
Man more than day
and less than words.
More days than work,
more work than things,
more things than help.
Years number men.
Men name home.
More names than homes,
more men than names,
more years than men.
More sound than thought,
more thought than world.
We see more than we can make,
make more than we can find,
find more than we can use,
use more than we can know.

I have one but what there can each like him see.

His Story

An old, old story,
to defy belief,
the darling child
spirited away,
and in his rightful place,
this changeling.

These toys were never his.
These rules were never his
to keep, or disobey.

These transparent people
never could be his,
even in this pallid light,
paling as they look at him.

They'd distract him with the stories:
how the son who slew his father
flourished in his wickedness,
how the son honoring his parents
flourished in his sickness.

How the honored father
went blind amid such glory.
How the blind man saw the light,
the pallid light, rejoicing.

The story of his murderer,
lacking means, enamored of his end.
Shadowed by the lovers,
enchanted with beginnings,
enchanted with the radiance
that blinds them to their ends.

Of the thoughtful man, who sees
all this, bemused
before beginning.
A story that won't stop,

as he's aware, a war
that's undeclared, besieged by thought.

Of the soldier, enamored of his wounds.
Of the deserter, enchanted by his fate,
to find each man's hand against him,

helping him. Of the teller of the tale,
too easy to believe him
enchanted with its outcome,
its familiar outcome.

Of the poet, enchanted, enamored & bemused
by others' words, those toys,
& others' tales, those rules
they mean to keep, & disobey.
The mocking, wistful poet.

But nothing can distract him.
The story of the fool
stumbling on the truth,
blinded by its radiance, a light
like that striking up off ice,
he warms to, but only till it's clear.

So they tell him
the hardest to believe of all,
the child sought everywhere,
the enchanted foundling.

Lawrence's Irritations

Naked to the sungod, he knows
those others in their rubbery ways to be
mere sunbathers, disintegrating

it's an old truth known here & there he tells,
everyone
becoming Lawrence, among
everyone.

Absolute Assertion #334

There is only the kiss,
your first, so absolute
who would move on from it?
Everything that follows
only means to be what it meant,
all you could tell it led to.

Y (An Imaginary Letter)

Dear Anon — we exchanged names but I never heard a word
    you uttered
to be honest, except Put some spit on it. I can't meet you
at the appointed hour tonight, is it
that the excitement is more than I
can stand, is even more intolerable when I think I will
than this hollow feeling, playing it safe?

You are preparing in our secret
rented room, in the next hotel we get to explore,
comparing fittings

because I will not name but touch
the gloss that bedside light predictably
lays on your hide, nothing is more naked
than the shoulders, but once begun

how should I stop now —
your belly
white, flat
as a secret to one who isn't in it
& who doesn't care, but
I care,

I stare, fixing the dim blue cords
that draw me so
back, you
must be the one to lay the vacuum
created by each undulating form eluding me
along the avenue beyond my knowing
for all the world as though I didn't know them
to be so similar each to each & you, so nearly
not totally particular in all their differences

but you, the thighs & only me between them, we are
& could be again together weren't we
& the hands, naked,
with the spikes straight through them —

*

—isn't the end of it, one evening
I'll find these metal pieces, with nothing but
what resembles rust around them &
discard them, then
it is the fingers will appear but shimmering
& this is why.

We've Seen the Expression of Those People

running to the hole they're shot in
We've seen Death knock them off their feet
That has been our privilege
You can't say we're not prepared
Though the footage was a little fuzzy
we got the general idea
as it piled them up in their particulars
then threw the earth in after them
and left us here
Each minute of the day
has its specific features
Everything throws its shadow.

It's the Same Only Different/The Melancholy Owed Categories

For Cecelia
who also dwells here

If Fate could be taken and given a twist,
If Justice could be taken and given a twist
   to squeeze from it all that wine,
   to squeeze from it something like wine
which causes a sensation like being kissed,
which causes a feeling like being kissed
   on the mouth by Swinburne and apostrophized as
     Proserpine
by Liberty with Her shift off, who would pine
for that lonesome trail where cluster those berries,
why then who wouldn't collect those deadly berries
   until he'd squeezed enough to give a drink to someone fit
     to be
   inducing a trance whose figures turn out to be
     shot back through time or turned into an owl?
    Piglet and Jahweh, Allah and Eeyore and Owl
among a host of daffodils performing their mysteries,
we all crave firsthand information of the mysteries
   first glimpsed in childhood drowsily,
   to assure Christopher Robin as drowsily
    he sucks on his thumb, of his acceptable soul,
    but fear them also, since each of us is a soul.

Every endless summer hurries in a fall
If Truth's a jeroboam and its imbibers fall
   glad to the Axminster as one, and the cloud,
   and no blue skyscape is forever free of cloud,
each wakes up to appears to spell the word all,
personally, I detest this habit that causes the word *all*
   to penetrate my head and wrap thought in its shroud
   as its shadow wraps thought in its shroud,
no rose is a rose is a rose :
then the poet (once sober) buries his nose in a rose
   blowing for him all alone where we wave

O.K., but nothing one looks at that doesn't wave
one another So long. Where those peonies
fare well—grandad's ninety-four, but those peonies
he grew year upon year and took to all the shows
privilege nurtures so as to win all the shows
owed their uncanny identity to artifice. We rave
(the odd gardener grumbles), incite hierarchs to rave
since we can't touch, and never blame this on our eyes
and forget how such primacy's due to all eyes.

At first everybody figured Beauty could never die,
Experts declared that Beauty would never die
and next, that She would. While they studied Her lips
while a voice said She would. Norwegian people's lips
share an inescapable resemblance. What do you mean, *Nej?*
The Unnoticed entered their ears. In Trondheim, <u>*no*</u> *sounds*
like <u>*nej*</u>.
And so it goes—whatever at the spring of likeness sips
Independently wealthy of what? No-one sips
who's not also a drink. No delight
grows thirstier to take delight
in advantage that isn't for others a shrine
in identity at any wayside shrine
to advantage denied. Given a tongue,
Very true, but the anomalous too has a tongue,
and when it speaks we shriek aloud and think it fine!
try to think without jumping : you'll say everything's fine,
it addresses us in the language of maybe and might
while ellipsis neglected mutters its maybe and might
and assures some of us we were born to be hung,
till anomalous martyrs from identical lampposts are
hung.

But As for Art

The motel is downtown. The time is now.
And from the lines
representing spears or darts
pointing at the animal, we gather
somewhat of ourselves. The lovers
are enacted, this time,
by ourselves, and all the world
wants what we are,
envies our nakedness and ease.
Knowingly or not, they circle
the tableau one storey from the street,
and set us at their center. But
some time has passed since then.
You left and never have come back.
I have come to see the centrifugal image too:
the lines that point out and away,
anywhere but at the animal,
the ecstatic animal, as if to say
it isn't there, as if to keep on talking
were to banish it from consciousness,
and all our love of company conspired
to overlook it. But as for art,
those lines are meant to go both ways.

Love's Way

Love shall find a way — it has!
declare it as you will:

how can she hear, where
can she be, tonight

and what will it mean to her
tomorrow morning?

So the Darkness

So the darkness has a voice.
So, for one to speak of it at all,
some density dwells there,
with breath to sound it out.

Let me call it you
since I have sensed you so.
Not that you spoke, that night in mind
knowing that wasn't called for.

But once you called my name,
holding me close.
Let me speak of this,
though it is not the same,

though it can never be the same
as you, in your darkness, know.
Penetrating there,
I had no thought of speech.

I had no thought. Your opening
sustained me, as I sustain
the blood within,
until it see the light.

Till then
I must speak on its behalf
of joy,
its joy.

Haven't we moaned for it,
imperative, against our densities?
You drew me into you
and said my name.

Laying the Word

It wasn't the Return of the Great Mother
it wasn't the Return of the Repressed,
nor being born again, nor was it yet
the Pure Experience of Otherness,
you laid the word on me & I responded,
I laid my hands on you & I had no defense.

Now what to call it, in our need,
this relationship we've launched,
this mutual agreement to be broken
open, this mystery that lifts us,
love, — if none of these suffice
they'll do, they'll say what I wants of you.

Finally

You will be a cipher for me
finally.
The dross of all associations
dropped away,
all errors of the flesh
in its expectancy, finally
shall perish in that hour.

Every assumption, each prediction,
proves its own
miscalculus.
All but one

drawing me to you,
consumed in touching
what but words create
finally, each time —

your body's face, your voice,
a code for me,
past all that's mine.

Poem

The mouth opens,
no words form.
A silent poem —

where poetry speaks
our joy & its
astonishment — in this
extremity I would surrender
all the words I know
to hear those few

to be the poem of you
known so. To open
the thrill in beauty loved.

And next to that
ecstasy, sensual release,
and passionate delight can go,
to its astonishment, joy too
I'd sacrifice, to gain
that text, that still

eludes my tongue.
Some god, goddess,
must be laughing up at me,

who could never bargain
except to take these words
and all they mean, & silence
them, to open —
the power of my own presence
thrills, I must confess

you are its instrument
alone, such power I know
brings me to silence, only

an opening in openness.

Prayer

To be with what we're with
and know it . . . in this meeting
of your eyes we recognize
this terror. And go on
looking. Afraid
to look away.

All error waits
for either glance,
ingrained in the twist
of carpet, a stain
of paint against a wall.
Of this place where
others tried to live.
Of others, all we know
stops short of this
place where,

by a twist, by stain
on stain, we two, who came to live
have, are, come to life. And life
that would go on

would falter over
what comes next.
For isn't this the prize
all would secure
we are, and have to,
and know we have to,
lose? If a prayer
would spare us,
give us courage so
to gaze and then let close
these eyes,

so be it —
opening once more
upon our reassurance,

we prayed to no-one
but ourselves —
or, in those eyes,
its cause.

A Shadow

We shall retreat, each from each,
our love, at last, withstood,
our semiology grown obsolete

that says, nothing lasts
for ever. And the poetry it wrote —
will it retreat from us

or like our memory, each of each,
that stays with each for ever,
cheat us — its hopeless lovers.

Gifts

Why nurse these grievances in loneliness
against lost lovers
for all the grief they caused—

what else enables one in going on
if not those tokens
lovers give, in being such,

one to the other? Now one
I may call you lights up
what I call my mind—

if only that you taught
how I couldn't call it yours,
and could. This loneliness

is all the surface
that your light requires.
And I praise what we've called love

for your presence in this world.
Wherever tonight you look
this world's not turned into a joke,

and I trust laughter discovers its relief.
Bliss knows I hope, the truth is suffered.
You gather brothers for my grief.

Recognized

Such a look you send
that courses through direct
on target — *recognized* —
a crowded room, all cliches
concerning love start up
what clamors for another
naming in my breast —

so that I chatter on
renewed — are these
people those our love
in its vital superfluity
needs flow out through
so justified to use —

were you not present
shouldn't I be dumb before
the longest-suffering
object of my intended succor —

how then did it happen, ever,
that we two came together?
What a makeshift world,
unuseable, hopeless
with its hazards,
the look you send
would not obliterate.

PART SIX
Developing the Negative

Tight Corners

Concepts protect one from experience: So she had conceived.

Along with the phone a device they had installed allowed them to turn down the bell. Should it be used, no matter how urgent or trivial the message, it would not get through, because they wouldn't hear the signal that preceded it. It would be as though they were out of the house, or in a coma, or dead. When they were dead news, no matter now alarming, would no longer concern them. But they were not yet dead, & so could move from place to place, raise their arms, bend the fingers, oppose the thumbs, & switch it off and on.

But a sentence, as the expression of a complete thought, is not natural & does not exist in nature. Is not natural & does not exist in nature.

Love is just around the corner. Any corner obscures one's view. Any corner constitutes one's view. How not to believe it is a right angle, although any intersection consists of 4 such, facing various directions. Love is a dense volume. All its pages have corners. Sometimes, as here, only words can be the means to turn them.

It all, he informs us, rests firmly on the edge of oblivion. Living on, we will not see his face again. I don't want to see what I shall never again see. I want to rest. That's why it all has to look permanent. He hasn't found rest, rest is a sentient occasion. He is permanent. I can alter his significance with every sentence.

Sitting in judgment on one's judgment. The wind moves by one in the grasses. How vague it is. How clear it might be. Who was one addressing. One's reflectiveness did one credit. Several possibilities occurred. One had recently left — someone who wouldn't allow one to be who one wanted, but instead, invented a person this someone wanted one to be. One would rather not receive another such visit. One did not like to be alone.

The scenario was rehearsed for a month in a stage-set replica of the objective on the Florida Gulf Coast. When we realized there was no-one in the compound, it was like hollering in an empty room, I had the most horrible feeling of my life. All the long training, the courage, the perfectly executed mission, had come to naught. The Secretary of Defense was moved to declare the affair a successfully completed operation.

Contemplating what had to be taken apart & erected, he sensed the imminence of despair. If only he were to make the materials somehow bigger, — stretched so that fewer of them would suffice. But on that rack would their information lose integrity? On that rack he himself would confess to anything, just to be done with it. What was needed was to keep the materials intact, stretching, instead, the edifice, so that it would have to contain more space than he'd supposed. Again, though, time itself could be stretched, that is, its integrity could be preserved, for in stretching it he meant only that the project should be longer. It could not be cut off by death because with each act of dismantling & reconstruction the whole assumed, once more, a final shape. So, then — it looked like everything was fine after all which was a relief because it was getting very late & he was mainly concerned with the evasion of despair.

Light is a shower of pebbles. Light is a shower of ripples. Light is a sower of parables. Light is a sewer of symbols. Light is white & might & sight & right, light has an endless appetite, until it looks like night.

She put her hand on him. She put her hand on him. She was confused. She is not to be confused with someone else.

He felt, sometimes apologetically, that he'd had a happy childhood. Then they told him about the isolation hospital. In 5 seconds his happy childhood had been wiped out. He began to understand something about the way he was.

The 80's are the 50's all over. I recall in the 50's a number of men who called their wives Mom. And I heard this again lately.

An angel stood before him in a vision & told him to catch the next number 87 bus. That had been just the bus he'd been waiting for! On the bus he found a penny. This meant he was going to get money. In the penny a man's face appeared. He was going to be president. At this, he got off. A sound too high for human hearing assured him no birds would be flying today. A flock of birds flew past. This meant war, R,A,W, means war.

The unconscious is an unlisted station on the Metro. No trains ever stop there. That's why the platform is so crowded. Yet whenever he descended there, he found it all attention. Something obscure was always vanishing, into the tunnel or out of it.

All the most brilliant periods of history flashed before his eyes as the sun glinted up off the straits. He was blinded momentarily & alone with some red & green dots & patches. But something that drummed in his ears reassured him. That was the ocean of his dreams.

As it fell out, he fell out of the train he chanced not to have missed, & by sheer good fortune landed in a passing river. He was fished out by a picturesque pair of gamekeepers who, unable to believe what their luck had brought them, realized he meant nothing to them & left him for dead on the bank. Here an occasional heiress revived him on a mere whim, not knowing what else to make of him. Already his will was to make the truth of his life the purely arbitrary.

Expressiveness is a myth. It is only the convention of expressiveness. How cold the real thing can sound.

I wanted to worship and you would do. I wanted to send you on ahead. I wanted to send you on a head on a platter.

Having thinking as my inferior function, I fell under the spell of Jung's "Psychological Types."

We can send someone in your place, they assured him. Great, & who was it? You, they replied.

One in Five Acts

When she returned home, nearly 2 hours after the time she'd led him to expect, he was quickly aware of something different about her—some alteration in her accustomed manner so subtle & so elusive as to be evident only to him, though even he couldn't put his finger on it quite yet. I've been fucking Ben, she said.

When she returned home, surely it was at least 2 hours after the time she'd named, he was aware, almost as though he'd expected it, of some subtle change in her accustomed manner, though only he, her husband of many years, would notice it, he supposed, as he studied her narrowly for the one clue more he needed. I haven't been fucking Ben if that's what you think, she said.

When she returned home, he studied her for some minutes, covertly, puffing on his meerschaum & with his other hand thrust deep into his dressing-gown pocket. His lean, hawklike features were a sight to see. I got my hair done, she told him.

But now—a rash on his hawklike penis!

She is sleeping. He raises the pillow & holds it just above her mouth & nostrils. Such impulses race through his system as can't be put into words. People shift uneasily. Who knows what he'll do next. He's forgotten his lines.

184

Everywhere he went he thought of her. Everything he did he did differently because of her. He could hardly wait for the next time. This had to be the doing of the god Amor. Now he had forgotten her phone number.

3 people whom she knew were coming up the lane. The sun was just setting. Their car was stopping at the stop sign. Now, as the wind was getting up, all the trees were beginning to whisper. One of them knew these people she knew elsewhere, where she had lately been, who had the treehouse. Now it grew dark. It was all a coincidence.

He thought it humanity's lot for ever to be persuading a huge rock up an alp, & at the top it would roll back down the same side, unaided. Those who would disagree with him were at liberty to remark the beauty of the meadows, the whiteness of the Edelweiss, & the unearthly peace of the pauses in this process, but not to deny they had rocks in their heads.

He washed up on a desert island, where he incurred the most remarkable series of mishaps that somehow kept turning out for the best. He had no time to keep a journal. He was never rescued.

If the workers were alienated, their so-called betters were doubly so. The society in its deadly way dragged on & on & nothing could redeem it short of a spiritual revolution to put men & women in touch with their immediate needs, so that what came to hand would show one where one's head was at. Her guru, whose ruminations this summary derives from, had performed one final miracle before dying, 30 years ago: he'd willed that no decay should disturb his much-loved form. Now she found herself in Tibet, cutting her guru's hair & fingernails.

My hero was no hero to this man. And understandably — as contemporaries, they had gone step by step into various misunderstandings that felt like betrayal. Well, but why couldn't this man understand how I must feel toward his dead contemporary? Maybe he did, & strove therefore to correct my impressions. He wanted me to see what my hero had taken exception to.

"Insurance can't buy me." She was splendid, head thrown back, lips pursed, male ticket torn into little pieces: how proud her father would have been had he been able to be present, the Beverly Hills multi-millionaire.

What worried him was, that he would not for long be able to put up with the ways life would be. Appealing as he found a number of people, not one but turned out discomfortingly weird in one way or another. What was it — as though some vast chord of madness had been struck on some unimaginable piano, & each was a wire, reverberating. The trouble was, that it *was* unimaginable. Not that he couldn't see it with some clarity — a darkwood upright floating somewhere between Mars & Venus, with a man in tails playing it, his patent-leather pumps at its pedals. But enough of facts. Why give so much of our belief to that which can be proven to be true? It was not *his* faith that was in question. He addressed himself once more to his visitor, & agreed that there seemed little likelihood of physical death destroying the essential character of the deceased. Then he asked him if he liked piano music.

Both rage & anger are extractable from Reagan & it is heartening news indeed that he manifests the latter over the latest Israeli attacks he might have encouraged in secret. "U.S. President Angry but Impotent." The hegemony prevents that headline. Reporters want to retain the privilege of receiving prepared non-answers to their searching questions. The heat is to be kept out of the kitchen (passive construction).

An evening like many he had spent, the lamps lit, a fire in the hearth, sweet night at the windows, its moths fluttering there. A white hair floated onto the typewriter. What was this utter sense of reassurance — none of this had ever happened before.

They sought, on a quantity of walls, the qualities of things that were not there, & ended by seeing them, but no longer knew the dates they represented.

Dates?

The branches grew at a certain angle in respect of the light. The trees bent away from the direction of the prevailing winds. He examined his fingers. Between each at the base was a small web from swimming. He brought them up close to his eyes. Now he could no longer see them. But between them he could still see the trees. They had a persistent quality. Soon it would be night.

Facts have overcome ideologies. This sacrifice of instinctual satisfaction for the benefit of some soldier unknown to me. Small coffin, put to this use. An entire infantry division supported by tanks reasons society doesn't wish to be reminded.

A thing of duty is a bore for ever. Constant contrast understates continuity. We count, & our sediments are stratified. Variation, exaggeration, & the bridge gives way before we can know that it was weakened. Oswald is obliterated over & over: are there any examples?

Hieratics: A Triptych

0

Here we see a street replete with unfeeling judgements & cruel deeds at the end of the earth.

Innocence decelerates marketable catastrophe, animal & plaintive.

A hammer falls, the faces of the workers freeze in astonishment.

That's how jewelry is made.

The chevrons may be decorative or descriptive.

Alert criticism eliminates phenomenon.

She glides lightly & seductively away, except for the soft oval.

Circles with dots may or may not be human heads. And what of the swastikas? Abstract space fillers, or starfish?

Over I,
the words of our mouths.

Mongols on ponies waist-high through the wheat & the alligator.

The education law banishing belief.

Vagabonds, jailbirds, existential sportscar drivers, mountebanks, merry pranksters, gurus, badtrip artists, bring-down dittos, organgrinders, anyone over 30, oregano peddlers, certain higher powers, burning questions, american prolixity, baseball as poetry, naked dancers from the finger lakes region with family trees wherefrom depends the herpetic apple of anomie, a bunch of blokes push their way forward. Souls unabsorbed returned to bodies.

Go where you want to go. Yesterday.

1

The bird emerging from behind the head,
& her trancelike expression, as well as the hollow bowl.
There are masks of human faces.
This goddess risks all to be mortal,
her parents on low stools in ashes,
men & things set in a sparkling brilliance.
Utterly.   Adoration.
And deep in the woods, Freud's granddaughter's hut,
gods with no name,
& up above, the pond, a loveliest azure, & the insistent swallows:
"Drink from me,
so be it!"
Light beyond all praise,
lolling on the railing,
opulent, slipping from boulder to awning,
filtering through, receptive,
impervious, undeniable.

So there *was* a covenant made with Good & into its orders *I* was
born. Following her father into the lowroofed cave, she notices
what a grown person obliged to stoop might easily overlook.
Groups of dots, club-marks, ladder-like patterns, hands based on
a desire to express a fundamental conception rather than attempt
to capture. The deaf grasses of the meadow. Her round head &
fawn body, tingling. The bearded, present, head: freshness in ap-
proach, concentration of expression mature as to style, virtuosity
thrills the catlike texture of hair, eyebrows & beard, sleek skin.

Their steps directed toward something which can no longer be
borne, ghost on a chair on a pool of some sky . . . Seated beneath
a sunshade, he watches a group of men busily weighing something
white. From the left the small winged figure flies toward her with
open mind. Caught up in the elastic of youth, a transparent ritual
significance in his left.

"From here on in, every blessed thing is in quotes,"
& her trancelike masks,
as well as the mortal brilliance.

2

As the enchanted day draws to a close, accompanied by a swarm of cupids, spawned in the nearby marshes, they move with studied assurance of actors who play role superbly & scratch that later. This playfulness, so free from dogmas & catspaws, is so obviously idealized as to still any gossip, beyond the locked gates. The goddess is one of several identities: bared, & the snakes may represent rather than divine . . . Nervous flickering strokes create everything excited. Even trees agitate, yet the whole is lighthearted, conveyed sketch-like, rapid statues & a steep overgrown staircase.

He had looked black but love would whitewash all. Liquor passes through the filaments of nerves. It's 4 o'clock. Each is a sign of a different complex idea. Pick up the bat & hit it with the bird. Eloquence, the fair sex, two prevailing beauties, rise in vain to find fault with these arts wherein Men pleasure To be. Culture glosses over & over Mortality.

> Think of the sound of laughter.
> Now watch the man drop the cheese.

Out of doors is no constraint. We see a cat cautiously stalking the flat forms . . . People naturally prefer to sit at their ease, in sheltered parks & gardens, as if the scene were under water, & the gods wished to lay knowledge by day, choosing the recipients more carefully: semblance deprives terror; theirs are broad vistas with irregularly-spaced tufts of hair. Unseen hands undoes light work. If a man spray his playmates with a length of hose, he is not that hose. If these men lack the beauty we expect of epic heroes, their movements have an expressive vigor & love will last forever, not in monuments. The curled-up dog is certainly pliable. This is how society now sees itself: as opposed to the somewhat stilted hi-flown world of travesty. Dionysus reclines in his boat, but why is he at sea? And with prettified features & a body at once slim & quite frankly great expanses of blue & green foliage? Art & Nature, debase the grim myth in twain, take on fixed contours, become material. Only then does the next fragment fit itself into place.

The shadow took on a variegated daguerrotype. India ink, with its all-inclusive range from palest gray to deepest black, contains all the colors of this world. The middle classes become wealthy in the things of their daily life. The dust, the dirt, the doghair, the despair, all sorts of remains of food strewn across the floor, each with its own impeccable shadow. Isolation from the outside world & nearly the most efficient police state. His eyes seem already lost in the other world, a livid light, replacing the transient with a more enduring to be appeased. An attempt to prevent the father reappearing? The weirdly-shaped garden rocks are a good indication, the tiny red spot on a stool. Trees seem as if the scurfy flesh of witches had been pulled over them. Looks good! he reflects. An effect of brilliance vigorously banned.

>   Plums blossom,
>   sparrows in the camelias,
>   bamboo,
>   asymmetrically.

Despite its isolated prominence, the tiny figure in red on the shelf is only here as one more aspect of nature. The view may well be one familiar during his many years of seclusion. Then there's the dust that settles in every crevice & mars the stone, prophesying the Church of Lateran falling, but by the saint upheld. Preach to the ignorant. Begging to the poor. Absent from his body, wearing a tunic of coarse brown serge, bound with a cord. Saints blaze in two dimensions in the sky, attenuate toward heaven — cardboard cutouts pasted to those silver clouds that seal all in while they roll away, preaching all things must pass & deserve to while he wanders beneath the new apple-leaves, tending the leper, name of Evidence, the squeak upon a blackboard. A halfwit spreads own garment for him to walk over. Bodies that seem capable only of slow ceremonial celestial gestures in an expanding space that inflates the illusion of unreality; marriage of Byzantium & Thibet; the individual has ceased to reach the end of the road, while smallscale reliefs, especially ivory & metal, continue their variety of content, style, & purpose.

This is a piece of a portable altar for private devotions while traveling.

This is the disappearance of monumental proportions.

This is etched in acid.

This is a scene that belongs to a cycle of the 4 seasons with birds & flowers, & something small clutching at him, imploring he thinks help, each with its own unimpeachable shadow.

4

Here we see a street replete. Innocence decelerates marketable catastrophe, animal & plaintive. It discards the judge & levels the plaintiff. So-&-so made me.

Here turns the spear of there.

Thousands march past, & are gone,
the one for whom I'm wrong
eternally among the throng!

A tatooed & subterranean first. Specific organization of scarcity.

The chevrons may be decorative or descriptive. Restricting principles selection discarded. The defenseless maiden is fully as appealing as the martyred saint. She glides lightly, & seductively oval. Lozenges indicate legs, whether of man or chair; circles with dots may or may not be human heads; if it were not for the fact that the boat is upside-down & that the biggest fish has seized the head of one of the men, we'd read this simply as a pattern. And what of the swastikas? Abstract space-fillers, or just fish?

What could I do? God willing.
By the rivers of Babylon
where I now supped
when I remembered Zion?

How sing King Alfred's song
in (wrong) Australia?

The words of our mouths
over I.

Vagabonds, discharged soldiers, jailbirds, escaped galley-slaves,
smiling colleagues, swindlers, mountebanks, pick-pockets, busy
competitors, gamblers, maquereaux, obedient officials, trained
swiss vultures, bulgarian umbrellas good for a laugh, certain
higher powers, cigars & garlic sausage, american prolixity bur-
ning questions, baseball as prose, a bunch of blokes push their
way forward.

Go where you want to go, yesterday.

The Terms

If animals can couple
what was human about us —

my body penetrated yours
more gently than a sword.

The Crux

We assume
what we can leave unsaid.
What can we assume —
one day we'll be dead.

Love-poet

Love as a grace tells only
partially its story.
It is a bargain also, hard
& driven. We speak of it
yet you despise the words
& all they'd arrogantly
aspire to give away —

as, speaking of our week together,
This grotesque week, you said,
&, of the car, how you need it chiefly
to cart me to your need.
And there's your need —

an appetite you once despised
I'd satisfy, despite the pride
resisting me, that must
despise itself, enduring,
to that end, the tedium
I can become during those interims
when appetite is stilled —

& I ride where you drive,
a graceless grotesque instrument
in love, & find my grace
reading to you what you mean to hear
in your despite.

Untitled

for Merleau-Ponty

As I asked
What is going to become
of us, one fact

escaped me, you
were listening for me
to complete a meaning,

and looking at me
was the fact I overlooked,
looking at you.

What . . .

What could be your grounds.
And bit by bit, intermitted
with absence by the night and day,
with hours of present silence,
gestures, some ambiguous, some
I thought not, with words
I'd sometimes recognize,
and otherwise, with sounds
that held me rooted, riddling
—I found out I was right.

To the Limit

1

The loathsome thing has kissed
& I have woken. I am wedded
to my death. What happiness

I knew in dreaming's
broken open, no act
I undertake is single

now. No thought
that doesn't darken
in this doubleness I didn't choose

but grew to see was true,
that my parents had given me away
at birth. I am talking so

since no way out is left to me.
Maybe I hope, the way that talk leads
back, to find once more

the means to sleep. I think
I pricked my finger & the pin
like any pain, was token

to tell how vulnerable I was
in being flesh, & being so,
at that I fell asleep. To dream

nothing but a life, mine,
as we mortals like to call it,
& such delight I had of it

I dreamed somehow its span
went on & on, its future
somehow as its past, yet

mysteriously better. I learned
by various mistakes
but more by what went right

so that the dream seemed
reasonable, & that hope
did help, I loved, my love

returned, I didn't think it
an adultery. Now
how can I pay back what my love

with me, spent helplessly —
what of it remains? This
fact I find I'm married to

can't reclaim what, in its grasp
seems lost. I must
submit, I see

for my own self's sake, with grace,
since submit I must,
for I do not worship pain.

Perhaps this pretty
poetry I mean to make
may make my peace with

fate? It's late,
later than I thought,
I want to sleep —

I want to think death
tolerable, since death
colors all my thought. I think

to lull him with my
yielding till he nods so I
may slip away. I'll

steal the pin he wears
to hurt me with & meet
my mortal love once more

as we met before, as if
in dreams, so brave
& open in our ignorance

we were — though
no cause to tell of this,
talk's cheap, those

who live as we did
alone'll follow me.
But some impulse keeps me talking

fitfully — why
do I want to isolate it,
why is it so difficult?

All living things must die.
Fruit ripens & drops off the vine.
Energy can never be destroyed.

It seems the dream talks on,
simply to be its evidence
& solitary witness —

as if the kiss had only partially
dispelled *its* power
the lips attempt to shake it off,

the lips that kissed, or were
kissed, which is it? What vow
truly to remember

shows me words
absolving me so
this becomes that dream

no thought of death
—a night-nurse shaking
anxiously her charge—

can break? that time
won't bear me on from
to an evening all these words

can't protect against
the presence of the thing
that gave them life.

2

This is that mode
which makes us slaves
more subtly than force or torture can—

this apparition of a voice
& self-effacing craft
together can suggest

you have the choice—
nobody's saying what you have to do,
these phrases placed just so

enact a confidence
that must be yours
since now you are alone,

they might mean variously
one of several messages that you,
decoding, thus disclose:

the agency of that decoding
must be also, you.
Presuming on a native curiosity,

they lead you on—
you, a life whose singularity
rejects those times before you were,

alive now in this language
lifted from the dead,
whose deaths together form

a further message, Live
now, as we
did not, not fully, not

enough, in our own time.
The voices
stop. Having said

never any more than
that was what they knew,
they would. The rest is

dreams, to us, who are
awake. Vivid
being dreamed, fragmented

& fading in the day—
we know better, pausing
to see where this has brought us.

I think, one says, that death
as it possesses thought
impels us into slaveries,

that anyone who sells us
means to look away from that
fact, can thus exact

the tribute of our thought.
In brotherhoods transcending death
see the frustrated need return,

Valpurgis of a Thousand Years—
I think this process
has gone on long enough.

Maybe the words themselves,
these close accomplices of liars,
bear the blame. Or syntax

an affliction of the brain
has crazed us
in its orderings

bent upon some end.
Such resistance
brings one courage ·

without which, who
could face a death
this dream of courage says

obliterates the dreamer
while he or she still lives.
In abject terror,

as old records show,
the human, as its legs,
that panic drove, give out

always has then fallen,
prostrate, to lie
weeping, on the ground.

No means, without a god,
to get onto your knees
& then get up. You

can't live on your knees.
Though in that posture life
passes itself on

as the sentences of chromosomes
begin to wake up death again
& all its wild conceivings—

that death will fix. The words
will not stay fixed, but go on
making meanings

beyond what one had thought to mean,
who could blame you
if you let them be? Writing

will make slaves of us,
in various ways, will
generate more meanings

than the truth we need
can need, I die, you
go on, alone—imperative

given this is true, to be
free, since, given this, each
already is, you

free to die away from
me, as I, from you—free
too, to face such freedom as

we choose, you
it may be in a dream I
cannot tell, I

in a dream of telling why
such dreaming needs to be, that truth
I am the slave of saves from me.

A Blessing

This angel's only passing through
where passing's traces resonate —
let it be blessed
whether I can scan or not
the corpus callosum

that's grown between the brains.
And speaking of it
worship uvular & velum
as one would the waters
below whose surface one can swim
& godbless the glottis
because one doesn't choke on one's own spit.
And bless the diaphragm
that keeps the stomach from the lungs.
Bless this air
that keeps the tissue of each lung
from cleaving to itself

& bless the air
that brings me news of syllables
And when I fill with presences I can't possess
whose lips my tongue'll never part
bless B for a beginning
because it's broken silence
& transformed what's less.

I speak of distances
since messages eat space
as it eats them
Bless centuries

that in their irreversible advance
reveal just how this has to be
another kind of psalm.
Then bless the language
that grows to be this instant
& since all blesings come from God
bless them.

A Spell

Dark, because dangerous,
dangerous since new,
dwellers underground because of undermine,
& the insides of bodies as of objects,
& since precious had meant metals,
thus small, because of gold:

Light, for all that can effect
as known, & fair
as long as beauty is agreed upon,
thus safe, the pun
implying reasonable,
in the open to be treated with

& small because they are,
the ones they have to lure
into the light, into their light,
the light themselves make up, to make it plain

—but that the thought is petrified,
cemented, cemetery, sticking by the /c/,
as if the stones of any city
demanded that itself be utterly destroyed,
since two of either kind would make one man,
& can, & can
convince him they have gone—

that stops me cold, unless I find
the tale has been mis-told, the emphasis
by some omitted law been shifted,

how they had to dance, to fetch them up,
& how their dancing was a frenzy
blent of terror that the ground would give,
& desperate suspicion that the ground would give
nothing, leaving them amid these stones

& how precisely then the others stepped
into their midst, how calming
the words they had to speak, This gem
of energy is not a gem, but energy
—yet then they had that gem—or, This is
simply forest for the play of sun & shade
is what you see, but thinking, this meant only
vacancy, they danced, so they kept coming

& surface, because light.

What Counts

I say the wrong thing
because I want so badly to have it come out right
because I want to be desirable to you
because you show me signs
that say I am. I want to win you by quick-thinkingness
& so I can, just name a time & place
meanwhile, keep talking, while you tell me this.

Love Was Once a Little Boy

for C.K.B. and J.S.P.

She is his mother after all
& so the spears he hurls at her
are torn from the wild grass.

As Now

It traveled through your hands
so recently—so long ago.
The brain peers back and forth
and groans. As it grows
dimmer, now diminishes.

The hands turn over stones.
Their happiness watches from its caves and loves,
and loves them for it. Those stones, those
tones are all it was, as now,
as now, where the rhythm of your turning,

where the rhythm of your turning is
all the life it knows, its cave
would hold your brain, its only light
—so recently, so long ago—
as recently, as long ago, as tight.

Desire

A statue in a park
around which in grass
the lovers lie

while a solitary girl walks by
with perfect features as the clock
on city hall strikes one.

An Excrescence

Though I am barely human
the logic of this tree
grows clear to me, no matter
I know it in the summer,

I know the winter in it too.
Light forces it. As boughs
so forced up & out, so roots
are driven into earth, a balance

even I can find.
Admittedly with spring
excrescences occur — & fall.
Love among us humans

never can be otherwise.
The will of those that love
drives into thought concerning what
thus drives them

— into poems even —
never can be more.
For I am barely human
while speaking with this tree.

Abstract

My desire precedes me
who am its shadow for the light
glows from beyond its further side,

the flame to burn this shadow up
when I am one with light.
And so I live as darkness

and would to this end be,
proof
that that flame flames, that object

interposes, absolutely solid.
I can't spare breath on happiness
nor any of its relatives, description

of this kind must be distraction.
For the god I am the shadow of

once seared me in that flame,
and sealed my lips. I hurt
to talk. My god
must prove my spokesman:

he adores the thing I am;
the flame, the glowing, happy flame,
and sets an obstacle between.

The Object

Years afterward
I cherished a black scarf
and would show it to close friends
and say, It once was hers.

I last saw you in April '55.
I found the scarf December '56,
working as a janitor,
in a city where you never were.

A cheap thing, unpleasant to the touch,
rasping, & thin. Some scent
persisted, cheap also,
as reminder of the girl,

a girl, unknown to me.
I felt dirty when I handled it.
Desolate, when I lost it.
You meant the world to me.

To a Pure Content

I'll tell how I aspire —
to be done with interference,
inference, with cues I am to send
seductively, with clues I am
to pick up & to riddle out,
keep your eyes fixed to the ground

I'll tell myself repeatedly,
present your ear,
say the least you can
that still can make it plain.
I've seen eternity
and how it leans on men & women
snarling emptiness in time.

I'll be done with such involvement,
in further lives, & furtive loves
or otherwise that thrive & find content
with no help from this tongue,
can come to grief, diverted
by exactitudes of hand & line & eye
that hide the bitter truth —

just such as I am done with,
hopefully. These hands
need only clasp themselves
for their aspirations to come true,
these eyes, so blue, can close,
to disclose all love can do.
I'll do the most to make my message plain.
No-one will fall in love with me.

Another Voice

I heard it, but it took a while.
People have an idea of this place
as quiet, until they've been here.

Kids ride motorbikes in & out the apple trees,
Sundays, there's all the traffic snarled downtown
where two state highways cross, city people
trying to relax, half-a-mile away

ten thousand chickens in force-feeders howling,
quail, shotguns, assorted hammering & sawing,
a jackass, jaybirds, dogs, a goat —

so those voices a man has in his head
must keep pace, somehow, with it all —

Why can't they walk, didn't God give them legs.
Why gun, gun, gun those goddam engines.
Why shoot what they won't eat
just because it's there.
Why can't these people stay home, fix up
whatever corner of the city each is stuck with.
Where are the churchbells, when I was a kid —
whose chainsaw's that, don't tell me it's the eucalyptus,
I don't want to see those chicken-shacks.

Should we go on buying eggs from there.
Whose dogs are those —

and still another voice,
You don't know what this means.

The three dogs had her on her knees,
Bob Porter's goat, blood at her neck & flank,
but ran off straightaway as we came up,
answering those sounds.

I Dreamt That I

I dreamt some land where no-one
spoke my language, so it took
more time than I can tell to get across,
and in that land, I was immortal.

And there it was we met.
You put your hand on mine
and I could speak & sense you
comprehend. And start to feel

I knew what you were saying,
that we should stay together,
until I'd learned to follow you
completely. And that I did,

I thought. Until one day
you led me where,
I knew, we'd hit upon that place
set aside for us to live together in

forever, where we would work
safe from interruption, to perfect this miracle —
I woke beside someone like you,
speaking a kind of english, laughing.

5 Poems (*Sea* to *Witness*)

1

the sea doctor loves you. You shout across the street
  we are closing the book on this arrangement
    glasses nailed to the wall
      the bulldogs left to fight all on their own
red may mean promise, love not mean love
  a still center prove a corpse
    the yellow monotony affording access
      defeating concentration. The phone jumped
because that way of putting it is desirable
  your letter gave me great pleasure
    but about then it started to rain
      rare coins upon therefore someone else
vicarious makes no sense to the child
  who misses your quiet voice every night

2

politics often mocks the last word
and to contradict may be affectation
an unmotivated command need not be arbitrary
the ford looked to us like no ford at all
now that the ice has melted and the flowers
you have traveled halfway through your quest
he writes openly for the great system
yet these summer fogs and the winds they justify
perplexed the bellies of those
stuck there that season, the season of peccadillioes
looking into infinity
all of which lacks interest
like a letter home to mother
with milk spilt over the pavingstones of ochre
and tealblue, you feel stupid
among the crudity and reach towards

3

he decided it was wrong to be stupid
   given his lack of tolerance for himself
      about then he was given the prize
         chains fixed under the box by pins
she inverts his problem at the piano
   he can recognize and function
      the past has a bullet in its head
         since the night before last with its
approximation of an ironing board to licentiousness
   knowing there's something behind it
      just the same, we could still remember
         the seafood was better last year
here are a bag of walnuts and a nickel
   a faint ebullition to give thrill a form

4

Categories are only approaches to what we are
and so are busses, trains, and income taxes
Does pleasure render us objective? Write soon
enclosing map and halfprice coupons or freebs
I only like what I can understand the wimp spoke
while the whisp smoked and the whip looked short
I am the text and I desire you so put it there
and shove it in and out I call that attention
not explanation that so often fails to please
while guaranteeing reassurance of the hapless sort
We like to see the stump where the axe split it
or any kind of an image really is easier than not
We tracked back from the clarity that pane
to its fragments that shivered together
Someone wants to assert an identity and why not
He writes because he does not want the words he finds

5

Having renounced the power to communicate
at one time inherent in our language
quit perusing this as a sample of your cultural obligation
for what we have here ate the itinerary :
Black Mtn Poets: dawn
NY Poets: 3 in the p.m.
The Beats: the following dawn, having been up all night
went seeking Experience, from tugboat to uranium mine
far too late, anywhere in the West it all equates
Everybody wears underwear or has elected not to
As drugs freeze the nose so names freeze the brain
holding the disgraced real world (Boston) at arm's length
the content of empirical illusion crossed with trepidation
you could have your ideas modelled by actual persons
The title's a white cane to the poet
picturing at the eleventh hour an imaginary witness

My Mother Died of Emphysema

However close we fashion truth
what we term life
& the fictions that we make of it
to try to live
no more resemble one another
than lungs resemble air.

The Death of Poetry

The bad news came.
You got thinner with each day
and less substantial.
The end in sight,
painful breathing from the next room
came and went throughout the night,
and with morning
much to our surprise
you were standing in the doorway
wearing a headdress of duckfeathers
and an oversize pair of British Wellys.
You were off to compete in the triathlon.
We said, "That's poetry for you!"

The End of the Stranger

I have just refused.
I have nothing to say.
I think that single instance would have satisfied me.
I couldn't stomach this brutal certitude.
I'd pictured myself in freedom
standing behind a double rank of policemen.
I knew that night was coming.
I have never liked being taken by surprise.
I could hear my breathing.
I made the most of this idea.
I hadn't done x, whereas I had done y or z.
I had to keep some order in my thoughts.
I might just as well have heard footsteps.
I was staring at the floor.
I must have had a longish sleep.
I was still right, I was always right.
I'd been waiting for this present moment.
I have never liked being taken by surprise.
I knew that the night was coming.
I couldn't stomach this brutal certitude.
I had to keep some order in my thoughts.
I'd pictured myself in freedom
standing behind a double rank of policemen.
I was still right, I was always right.
I hadn't done x, whereas I had done y or z.
I might just as well have heard footsteps.
I have just refused.
I think that single instance would have satisfied me.
I could hear my breathing.
I have nothing to say.
I must have had a longish sleep.
I'd been waiting for this present moment.
I was staring at the floor.
I made the most of this idea.

Snarling Traffic

Your mind in showing
decent interest lost
no time in crowing—
some ingenious person's
elementary way. A dis
tinguishable series of
events is precisely that
we're after. Corrosions
of conversations, cautious
expressions of the trans
cendent instance. "By
the way, I think I'll
change my mind." *Tak
so mycket*, & so talkative,
we know just what to say.
Schooling nodded
confidently. Any true
signature misses the
impression it makes.
My altruism meets
your selfishness in
identical rivers of
elite landscape where
we say our own mouthfuls
tasted elsewhere.

Zeno's Present

Those were the days.
I am taking your place.
All that talk of passion,
black leotards, we have some
fine words here. Writers all
reserved . . . Found, ratified, proved
right, delivered over to tomorrow, by
the phrase "never mind about my life" —
an excuse to write never mind. Nimble and
oblique, having that in common. Cranking up.
Doubts, thrills, important papers gone to dust,
the human element, umm, Thanks. Figuring the moon
snagged in the branches of successive trees moved in
accord with him — perception an art analogous art per
ception. Quaint, all these who scarcely can be thought
to care. God, gold, pretty words in general: travesty, thester
nesse, crepuscule, nightingale, tanktop. Emotions in terms of minerals,
product, wallpaper landscapes. Once upon a time and then to hell in a
handcart. Hold, rock, chant, locked in with an object
for then one has time to consider, in 3s or 7s, or
the sidewalk between trees. Make housework a song.
Famous last words: no more irony. Take it away.

The Logical Positivist

Has painted his hands blue
to disturb assumptions perhaps
but more credibly, to pass muster
at the costume St. Valentine's party

he attends clad in the same drab
we identify him by in the Philosophy
Dept.'s corridors, & is about to dance
all night with your date, an enthusiast

naive, who finds herself fascinated
by his brusque request for sex & the lake
(after all, mainly ornamental) to stay
calm. Much later, weeping, this beauty

will return to you insisting
she was too young to know
a heel when she held one in her own
pulsing embrace, & that flowers

(for isn't she a dilly) don't open
overnight, an obvious contradiction
given the condition of her corsage.
Either way, reject her or accept her

pathos, he wins. Except
your fantasies can't matter
to him, & so he hasn't
triumphed over you, rendered

ridiculous now in yellow (not
your most flattering color), the necessary
outfit if you want to go as a jingle
(her idea) from an old toothpaste ad.

(She wore yellow too, a knock-out
with eyes of cornflower blue & skin
so fair of hue the feelings
register immediately as the heart

sends blood wherever ordered to.)
Say he undressed her, he undressed
anybody. Told her she didn't exist
per se so she took her costume off.

We sat on the stairs to the cellar,
I didn't know what to do. Later,
(years go by), he was recalled
as a bitter twist in speaking,

a mordant humorist, one of your
pas sourir bespectacled
numbers — he enjoyed a drink
one heard: feel that slide down!

"The basic condition of our ideation
comes to this: universal facticity
vs. hierarchy, but if the latter,
by whom declared?" So at last

we come to *you*, not that I
think it essential to proclaim
the presence of a person in a construct
someone had to make; no, nor conceal.

What they think of me
stays a problem in identity.
The occasion of their fancies
salutes them, but not I.

We laugh at free will trapped
in a mechanical model, unable
to prevent ourselves. Meanwhile,
she marries a third fellow,

has five children, lives in a converted
windmill, & you . . .
were always too young for what occurred,
that's why this burrow was provided

to drag yourself & its remains
into, rare subterranean
ruminant disguised as a suburban
unit in the Year (& what isn't)

of the Irresistible Force.
People pay for answers not questions
around here. This is, it has no, end,
high spirits. Indicating that praxis

wherefrom we abstain: the creation
of just life, for considering the
relation between style & the unfamiliar,
those who have nothing to say

are those who count eventually.
This is the party, no more speechifying,
come as you are, representing
more than you ever dreamed

of witnessing under the Japanese
lanterns to disgraceful strains
the dancers whirl to, upended on the water's
surface, whose depth's not yet decided, never was.

At midnight, out of it
emerges this furious
creature of unfashionable drama
crying "Glorious excess,

uncalled-for arrangements!
It's going to be all right!
It hurts so good! God bless!"
Language lets the ripples lap the edge

then recoil: or recoils;
all instances are final, none
evades decisiveness nor breaks
its circuitry; what else is death to do?

Sonnet

In a trackless wilderness, whence
this sense of lost ways? Next.
This is the same slide. Stepping
into the frozen frame of a river,
repeating patterns at each ankle.
Woozy nudes in the oozy woods. This
could be that bed of roses spoken of

so often pointedly by persons who
resemble blossoms and also the wind
that scatters these. I who change
constantly fled them lest I be by them
caught and killed that each might keep
unchanged. A dream can be neater than
we think. I know what I like

isn't art. He burned his hands
badly trying to gold lead — an
all-around genius. Were faith

greater it would destroy its application.
A methodology of doubt must yield at times
and pain chide the beast it rides upon.

Printed July 1988 in Santa Barbara & Ann Arbor
by Graham Mackintosh & Edwards Brothers Inc.
Design by Barbara Martin. This edition is pub-
lished in paper wrappers & in a hardcover trade
edition; 150 hardcover copies have been numbered
& signed by the poet; & there are 26 lettered
copies handbound in boards by Earle Gray each
containing an original drawing by the poet.

Photo: Christopher Bromige

David Bromige was born in London, England in 1933. He earned degrees at the University of British Columbia and the University of California, Berkeley. He is Professor of English at Sonoma State University and lives in Sebastopol, California.

He is the author of such notable books of poetry as *The Gathering* (Sumbooks Press, 1965), *Threads* (Black Sparrow Press, 1970), *Birds of the West* (Coach House Press, 1974), *Tight Corners & What's Around Them* (Black Sparrow Press, 1974), *My Poetry* (The Figures Press, 1980) and *Red Hats* (Tonsure Press, 1986).

David Bromige's impatient imagination has refused fashion for more important goals in the poem, often writing beyond our ability to recognize how wonderful and witty his creations. . .because we were so struck by how *true*.

—Ron Silliman

This new collection of poems which is traditional without being old fashioned seems particularly in keeping now with a time in which we want grave reflection rather than drama.

—Diane Wakoski

Very few poets have watched their own poems unfold with such mordant and skeptical intelligence. *Desire* is nervy and bracing work, not easy to enter, and deeply suspicious of easy entry, but it is that suspicion, impatient, ironic, amused, that gives the book its originality and edge.

—1988 Western States Book Award Jury

The intelligence of these poems is a singular delight and authority. Here are all the active resources of thinking the world as the human place it must be—no matter what we think. Thank *Bromige* for making it so!

—Robert Creeley

A truly original book. Narrative and lyric fuse to create new configurations of great density. Bromige's language is extremely rich and elliptical; his images take us into a world where things happen mysteriously and often frighteningly—and it is to us that they happen!

—Marjorie Perloff